W9-ADZ-821

ALCTS Papers on Library Technical Services and Collections, no. 4

.M28
F67
1993

Format Integration and Its Effect on Cataloging, Training, and Systems

---

Papers presented at the
ALCTS Preconference
"Implementing USMARC Format Integration"
American Library Association
Annual Conference
June 26, 1992
San Francisco, California

edited by
Karen Coyle

series editor
Edward Swanson

DISCARDED

Research Center
Wisconsin Veterans Museum
30 W. Mifflin Street
Madison, Wisconsin 53703
Ph: (608) 267-1790

American Library Association
Chicago and London 1993

Cover designed by Jim Lange

Composed by Digital Graphics, Inc. in Helvetica Narrow and Times
and set on a Canon XBP900 imagesetter

Printed on 50-pound Finch Opaque, a pH-neutral stock, and bound
in 10-point C1S cover stock by IPC, St. Joseph, Michigan

The paper used in this publication meets the minimum requirements of American National
Standard for Information Sciences—Permanence of Paper for Printed Library Materials,
ANSI Z39.48-1984. ∞

Library of Congress Cataloging-in-Publication Data

Format integration and its effect on cataloging, training, and systems
/ edited by Karen Coyle.
   p. cm. — (ALCTS papers on library technical services and
collections ; no. 4)
  Includes bibliographical references.
  ISBN 0-8389-3432-3
  1. MARC formats—Congresses. 2. Cataloging—United States—
Congresses. 3. Cataloging—United States—Data Processing—
Congresses. I. Coyle, Karen. II. Series.
Z699.35.M28F67 1993
025.3' 16—dc20   93-19721

Copyright © 1993 by the American Library Association. All rights reserved
except those which may be granted by Sections 107 and 108 of the Copyright
Revision Act of 1976.

Printed in the United States of America.

97 96 95 94   5 4 3 2

Contents

Contributors to This Volume

Jo Calk is Library Applications Programmer at WLN. Her previous library experience includes serving as Senior Automation Planning Specialist at the Library of Congress and as Authorities Librarian at Cornell University Library. She is a past chair of the LITA/RTSD/CCS Interest Group on Authority Control in the Online Environment Ad Hoc Committee on Linking Bibliographic and Authority Records.

Priscilla Caplan is head of the Systems Development Division of the Office for Information Systems in the Harvard University Library. She is LITA representative to the MARBI Committee, 1990-93. She is responsible for the Format Integration changes to Harvard's locally developed library system, HOLLIS.

Karen Coyle is Technical Specialist for the University of California's MELVYL system, where she performs systems analysis for the building of bibliographic databases. She is a past chair of LITA's Programmer/Analyst Interest Group and was LITA representative to the MARBI Committee, 1989-92. She has published articles on a variety of topics, including bibliographic record matching and Format Integration.

Richard Greene is Senior Consulting Database Specialist at OCLC. He has been OCLC's representative to MARBI since 1980 and has attended all of the MARBI meetings dealing with Format Integration. He is also Product Manager for OCLC's implementation of Format Integration.

v

Anne L. Highsmith is NOTIS Coordinator at Texas A&M University. She has served on the MARBI Committee for several years in various capacities, culminating in chairing the committee in 1991-92. She has written articles on system design for technical services functions and the human/machine interface.

Derry C. Juneja is Chief of Technical Services at the Riverside City and County Public Library, Riverside, California. She served as chair of the Speakers' Bureau for the Council of Regional Groups of ALCTS, 1990-92, and was the CCS representative to the Public Library Association Cataloging Needs of Public Libraries Committee until 1993.

Laura Kimberly is Training and Support Manager at the AMIGOS Bibliographic Council, Inc. She is the 1992-93 President of the Continuing Library Education Network and Exchange Round Table of ALA and currently serves on the OCLC Network Coordinators MARC Format Integration Training Task Force.

Sally H. McCallum is Chief of Network Development and MARC Standards Office at the Library of Congress. She has worked in various ways with USMARC and its integrated international counterpart, UNIMARC, for more than 15 years. She headed the office that is responsible for the U.S. format during the entire Format Integration development process, serving as the Library of Congress liaison to the MARBI Committee.

Glenn Patton is Senior Consulting Product Support Specialist at OCLC. He serves as OCLC's representative to the ALA Committee on Cataloging: Description and Access and is a past chair of Online Audiovisual Catalogers. He was a voting member of the MARBI Committee during most of the Format Integration discussions.

Paul J. Weiss is the Systems Librarian in the Office of the Chief of the Technical Services Division at the National Library of Medicine in Bethesda, Md. He was formerly the Monographs and Computer Files Cataloger at Mann Library, Cornell University, in Ithaca, N.Y. He has served as a member of ALA's Subject Analysis Committee and as a liaison to the Committee on Cataloging: Description and Access and currently reports on MARBI meetings in the LITA Newsletter.

Introduction

Karen Coyle

Format Integration and Its Effect on Cataloging, Training, and Systems grew out of the Preconference on Format Integration organized and sponsored by the ALCTS/LITA/RASD Committee on Machine-Readable Bibliographic Formats, known as MARBI. The preconference, held in San Francisco, California, before the 1992 ALA Annual Conference, sold out its 150 openings far in advance of the conference date. Three more sessions with similar content to the preconference are scheduled for 1993.

Yet, as we contemplated our success after that first session in 1992, we were also painfully aware that these additional sessions would not be sufficient to reach the many librarians who need to know how Format Integration may affect them. This book is an attempt to bring the essential information about Format Integration to that larger audience.

The chapters are based on presentations from the preconference, but the authors have made revisions to make them more suitable to the print medium. Some information, such as specific information on the plans and progress of the various utilities and vendors, was considered too volatile for a print publication and is not included here. Vendors will provide updates for their systems as they implement Format Integration.

If it achieves its purpose, this publication should give you a sense of how Format Integration will affect your library and its activities and should help you begin planning for that change. It provides an overview of Format Integration and its history, discusses its effect on cataloging and systems, and explores issues in training and documentation. Each section speaks in a general way about what one can expect of Format Integration; each library will need to apply these concepts to its own operations. If you find yourself frustrated at the lack of pat answers to some of the questions raised by the authors, please remember that while we understand the principle of Format Integration, none of us has real experience with it yet. We will gain that experience together as we all begin to use the integrated USMARC formats.

As you read this book, you will perceive some differences of opinion among the authors on certain aspects of Format Integration. We hope these different points of view will stimulate your own thinking on the topics presented. Some of these may be clarified easily after implementation; some may lead us to yet other enhancements to the USMARC formats.

I cannot encourage you enough to begin thinking about and planning for Format Integration as soon as possible. The reassuring theme that recurs through these pages is that much of what you do today will not change when Format Integration is implemented. Identifying those areas of your library operations that will be affected is the best way for you to be comfortable with the upcoming changes and confident that your library will be in step with the greater bibliographic universe in which we operate today. I think you will find, on analysis, that Format Integration is a relatively simple task. Perhaps, as Jo Calk suggests, you can even begin to think of it as an "opportunity."

This book is truly a collaborative effort, beginning with the efforts of the organizers of the preconference, especially Kathy Bales of the Research Libraries Group, who was then chair of MARBI and the motivating force behind the preconference planning. I wish to thank each of the authors included here, who not only participated in the preconference but also were willing to undergo the work needed to prepare their preconference talks for the print medium. Of the authors, I give special mention to: Jo Calk, who gave me many good comments on the first draft; Glenn Patton, who rewrote the introduction to the cataloging section on a moment's notice; and Paul Weiss, who did extensive editing of the cataloging section and the examples.

On the home front, I am greatly indebted to Mary Jean Moore (University of California, Library Automation) for detailed editing of the texts included here. If there is a voice that carries through these diverse documents, it is attributable to her skills as an editor.

Technical Notes

This document, by its nature, makes some assumptions about the technical knowledge of its readers. In particular, it is assumed that readers are familiar with the *Anglo-American Cataloguing Rules*, second edition, and with the coding of USMARC records. At the same time, it is acknowledged that the frequent reference to particular USMARC tags may make this document difficult reading and that it would be a great inconvenience if the texts here could be read only with an open copy of the *USMARC Format for Bibliographic Data* constantly at hand. To that purpose, at the first mention of each USMARC tag in each chapter, we have included the name of the tag from the USMARC format documentation:

... field 246 (Varying Form of Title) ...

Throughout the book, the terms "Leader" and "008 field" are used as defined in the *USMARC Format for Bibliographic Data.* Because most non-systems librarians do not know these fields under these names, a short explanation is necessary. The Leader is a 24-character field that appears at the beginning of a MARC record and contains information that allows computer systems to process the record. Most of the elements in the Leader, such as record length, are system-generated; the average user never needs to see them. Two of the Leader elements are assigned by record creators, however; these are the Type of Record and Bibliographic Level.

According to the definition in the *USMARC Format for Bibliographic Data,* the 008 field "contains 40 character positions (bytes 00-39) that provide coded information about the record as a whole and about special bibliographic aspects of the item being cataloged."[1]

OCLC identifies the combination of Type of Record and Bibliographic Level from the Leader and the 008 field as the "fixed field." RLIN refers to the same combination of fields as the "fixed field segment." WLN's "fixed field" consists of field 008 and the descriptive cataloging form (byte 18) from the Leader; they display the Record Type and Bibliographic Level in their "header."

The appendix is a table of the Leader and 008 field positions as they are displayed in the RLIN, OCLC, and WLN systems. Glossary definitions of some of the terms that might not be in everyone's technical vocabulary follow.

Note

1. Library of Congress, Network Development and MARC Standards Office, *Format Integration and Its Effect on the USMARC Bibliographic Format,* 1992: 3.

Format Integration: An Overview

Anne L. Highsmith

The Need for Format Integration

Although, to some, Format Integration may seem a new and unfamiliar topic, the need for Format Integration was recognized more than a decade ago. By the early 1980s, it was clear that developing and maintaining formats separately created some difficult, if not insuperable, problems. First, catalogers found that many items were "un-catalogable" because they didn't fit into a single MARC format. As a Library of Congress staff member commented at a midyear MARBI meeting in 1983 in reference to a pile of serially issued films, "I can't catalog these. You've got to do something about this." Technically, of course, the problem was not that the items couldn't be cataloged. AACR2 allows the cataloger to choose rules from the serials chapter or visual materials or wherever as needed to compose a full catalog record. What was impossible was putting that composite catalog record into a MARC format, because format structure forced the cataloger to use either the Serials format or the Visual Materials format. The cataloger had to choose to represent either the serial or the visual aspects of the material, but not both. This led to inconsistent treatment, as catalogers made different choices about the same material. Inconsistency and incompleteness reduced the value of shared cataloging and ultimately impaired the usefulness of these records in online catalogs.

On the systems side of the ledger, the costs of maintaining and developing separate formats were also becoming very high. As one example, most systems contain validation tables for the USMARC format tags, indicators, and subfield codes. There was a great deal of unnecessary overhead in keeping separate tables for each format because of the large amount of duplication. Multiple formats also meant format-specific display programs, index routines, and a variety of duplicate processes in which there were more similarities than differences. By condensing the seven bibliographic formats into one, Format Integration allows systems to treat all bibliographic records the same way, thus reducing the costs of implementing changes to the formats.

Format Integration also eliminates the need to build a new format from scratch when material types are added to the USMARC family. With a single format, it is necessary only to add material-specific fields, rather than to consider every existing field for possible applicability.

Designing Format Integration

As a preliminary to investigating the feasibility of Format Integration, the Library of Congress and the MARBI Committee of the American Library Association agreed upon a rationale on which to base the integration process. This statement was adopted at the Midwinter 1984 MARBI meeting as the guiding principle behind Format Integration: "The USMARC bibliographic formats are considered a single integrated format. Content designation defined therein is valid in any record in which it is appropriate." [1]

In the final result, this meant that the format-specific validity tables would disappear. But, the tables could not disappear immediately—rather, they had to be eased out of existence by reconciling inconsistencies in the formats. This process of reconciliation and consolidation, which was carried out by the Library of Congress and MARBI during 1987 and 1988, was informed by two additional principles: (1) the same information must be treated the same way for all material types, and (2) the integration process must be carried out responsibly, retaining as much of the current structure as possible without invalidating any more existing records than necessary.

Seriality, Control Fields, and the 006 Field

The most difficult issue confronting those who were designing the integrated format was how to resolve the seriality problem. It was easy to declare that all tags could be used for all material types, but the same solution could not be applied to field 008, the coded data field, because it is nonrepeatable.[2] Following the principle of responsible integration, it was clearly impossible to make field 008 repeatable simply to solve the dilemma of the "uncatalogable" serials. Tempting as it might be to give that serially issued film two 008s, one for its serial aspect and one for its film characteristics, it simply was not possible in a world that had built systems on the nonrepeatability of that crucial field. The solution was to leave the 008 field nonrepeatable and add a field, 006 (Fixed-Length Data Elements—Additional Material Characteristics), that could be used to record the codes associated with the other identity of the material.

Under the old system of seven separate bibliographic formats, there was no confusion over selecting the appropriate 008 field because Record Type and Bibliographic Level determined which 008 field could be used. If the Record Type was coded "a" for Language Material, and the Bibliographic Level was coded "m" for Monograph, then there was only one set of 008 codes that could be used—those that applied to the Books format. Under the new system of all fields being valid for all formats, catalogers may wonder whether those rules have changed. Is this one of those areas where the cataloger is free to choose? The answer is a qualified "yes"—the cataloger may make a choice once certain basic requirements are met. The following model (Figure 1) prescribes how to select the 008 field for the USMARC record.

The first level of choice is prescribed: if the item is textual, choose from group A; if it is nontextual, choose from group B. However, some judgment can be exercised when selecting within a group, particularly for visual materials. When cataloging a multimedia item, the cataloger selects the 008 field that corresponds to the medium or aspect that he or she chooses to emphasize.

Fixed-field elements for additional aspects of the material are represented in one or more 006 fields. There are seven types of 006 fields, one for each 008 field type. Field 006 uses a tree structure, like the 007 (Physical Description Fixed Field) field, so that the first position (byte 0) contains a code that defines what type of 006 field it is and the remaining bytes are interpreted based on the value of byte 0. Bytes 1-17 of the 006 field contain the material-specific coded information that would appear in bytes 18-34 of the corresponding 008 field. Take the example of a serially issued film. Because it is a nontextual item, the cataloger codes a visual materials 008 field and puts the codes in the fixed field or equivalent, then codes the serials-specific elements from a serials 008 field and places them in a 006 field. Figure 2 below correlates the 006 type with its corresponding 008 type and presents the tree structure used to identify the 006 type.

If an item is basically textual

  Type of record = a (Language material) *or*
           p (Mixed material) *or*
           t (Manuscript language material)
  Bibliographic level = Any valid code
  008 = Book or serial or archival control
  006 = Any that apply to main item or accompanying materials

If an item is basically nontextual

  Type of record = c (Printed music) *or*
           d (Manuscript music) *or*
           e (Printed map) *or*
           f (Manuscript map) *or*
           g (Projected medium) *or*
           i (Nonmusical sound recording) *or*
           j (Musical sound recording) *or*
           k (Two-dimensional nonprojectable graphic) *or*
           m (Computer file) *or*
           o (Kit) *or*
           r (Three-dimensional artifact or naturally occurring object)
  Bibliographic level = Any valid code
  008 = Music or map or visual materials or computer file
  006 = Any that apply to main item or accompanying materials

Figure 1. Model for selecting the 008 field

Adding 006 fields to represent other identities of the item being cataloged is not restricted to the main item. These 006 fields also may be added for accompanying material or for the several items in a kit. Since selection of a particular format no longer locks catalogers into a list of possible 007 fields, they can also use multiple 007 fields to represent the physical description of the main item and accompanying material or kit members. If cataloging a book with an accompanying sound cassette, for example, the cataloger would select a books 008 field but could also include a 006 and 007 field for the sound cassette.

  The codes listed under byte 0 of the 006 field correspond to the codes that will be valid for Leader byte 06 (Type of Record) after Format Integration. A few additions and changes that resulted from discussions on Format Integration that took place at the 1988 and 1989 MARBI meetings have been made. Questions of how to code Type of Record and Bibliographic Level and what those two terms really mean made it increasingly clear that the concept of archival control, which had previously been included in Type of Record, was a separate entity, equal in importance to the other two. Any textual or nontextual material types or any monograph or serial bibliographic levels may be

006/008 Type	Byte 0 of 006	Material Type
Books	a	Language material
	t	Manuscript language material
Serials	s	Serial control
Maps	e	Printed map
	f	Manuscript map
Music	c	Printed music
	d	Manuscript music
	i	Nonmusical sound recording
	j	Musical sound recording
Visual Materials	g	Projected medium
	k	Two-dimensional nonprojectable graphic
	o	Kit
	r	Three-dimensional artifact or naturally occurring object
Computer Files	m	Computer file
Archival Control	p	Mixed material

Figure 2. 006 field tree structure[2]

controlled archivally. Thus, with the implementation of Format Integration, an additional Leader byte, byte 8, will be coded for archival control.

As an example, the UCLA Film Archive, if cataloging an archival collection of TV news shows, would code Type of Record "g" for Projected Medium, Bibliographic Level "c" for Collection, and Type of Control "a" for Archival Control. There also will continue to be an Archival Control 008 field, but this will be appropriate only for Type of Record "p," Mixed Material. This code is intended to describe mixed collections, not kits, in which "no one type of material in the group is emphasized or predominates. . . . This category includes archival and manuscript collections of mixed types of materials, such as textual materials, photographs, and ephemera."[3]

Variable Data Fields—01X-8XX

Once the seriality problem was solved, the MARBI Committee examined the variable data fields. Any USMARC content designation that was unique to a particular format or subset of formats was considered for extension to all material types. Any situation in which there was an inconsistency, such as an indicator value being valid for one format but not for all, had to be resolved. As a result of resolving inconsistent usage, several USMARC designators were made obsolete or deleted, or their use was redefined. A data element is deleted only when there is certainty that it has very rarely or never been used. The deleted element is removed from USMARC format documentation and the designator may be reused in the future with a completely different definition. For example, field 330 (Publication Pattern) was deleted because it had never been fully defined and currently is covered by the *USMARC Format for Holdings Data.*

Items that are marked obsolete remain in the format documentation and will continue to be processed in old records but are no longer valid for input into newly created records. Examples of fields that were made obsolete during Format Integration are field 211 (Acronym or Shortened Title) and field 214 (Augmented Title). Finally, field 740 (Added Entry—Variant Title), which used to apply to all title added entries in the nonserial formats, was redefined for use with analytical title added entries only. The rest of the fields that were previously tagged 740 now will be tagged 246 (Varying Form of Title). The complete details of these changes are included in the publication *Format Integration and Its Effect on the USMARC Bibliographic Format.* [4]

System Changes

Obviously, this new structure will mean changes in online catalogs, in catalogers' procedures, and in system design. The initial investment in training and reprogramming will be substantial. It will be useful to examine how these groups will benefit and what will be required of them to cope with the changes.

Examining the question first from the public services perspective, reference librarians will question how Format Integration affects their ability to retrieve materials, especially in those systems that allow them to limit searches by format. The answer is that all the information that could affect retrieval is still in the record, and there is nothing inherent in the concept of a single format that makes retrieval by type of material impossible. Like many aspects of this process, its ultimate effectiveness is determined by the way individual systems implement the integrated format.

Under Format Integration, the user will be able to retrieve on all appropriate aspects of all works when using a system that allows retrieval by format. The music historian now can find all music printed in Austria in the last quarter of the nineteenth century, regardless of whether the music was issued as a serial or as a monograph, and the scholar studying the history of European publishers can research serial publications and find all of them, not just the ones that happened to take the form of printed text. Integration should expand the ability of libraries to make their online catalogs into research databases.

Cataloging Changes

As for the cataloging process, the changes that Format Integration introduces will not cause catalogers to revise many of their established practices. The cataloging process remains essentially the same, as the cataloger decides what the focus of the item is, composes an appropriate description, and then assigns USMARC tags to that description. The focus of the description determines which 008 field will be used, and the full range of variable field tags is available to identify what has been composed. As for learning the details of the integrated format, this will not be a massive task once catalogers conquer the psychological hurdle of all fields being valid for all types of material. Fears have been expressed, for example, that catalogers will be forced to learn legions of new tags for which they have no possible use. These fears, like the rumors of Mark Twain's death, have been greatly exaggerated.[5]

The best criterion for deciding whether a specialized note tag should be used is one of simple reasonableness. Monograph catalogers, for example, have always used field 500 (General Note) to identify the language of a book, but now field 546 (Language Note) is available to them. Because it is reasonable that the specialized tag be used to identify the language note that would be made anyway, field 546 should be used to identify the language of the book. On the other hand, it would probably not be reasonable or useful to begin using field 511 (Participant or Performer Note) to list conference presenters because it is not part of normal cataloging practice to include such lists in bibliographic records. Catalogers must, as always, be guided by standards, the usefulness of the information they are providing, and good sense.

The changes, of course, come not in cataloging but in the encoding. In my opinion, the following represent the major changes for catalogers:

1. Catalogers of multimedia material, including nontextual archives, now will have the necessary freedom to do a full description and include coded data elements for all aspects of materials.
2. Monograph catalogers and catalogers for textual archives will be able to bring out secondary aspects of materials by including coded data for accompanying material and ephemeral items. In addition, such catalog-

ers will have to learn some new notes fields and when to use field 246 versus field 740.

3. Catalogers of textual serials will see the least change. Many obsolete serial fields and coded data elements have been dropped, and in the few conflicts between monographic and serials practices, such as using field 246 versus field 740, or the 008 date type codes, the conflicts were resolved in favor of retaining serial practice and redefining monographic practice.

Obviously, there will be a learning curve as the above changes are implemented and certain specific decisions are addressed. Now that it is possible to include a wealth of coded data, is it truly desirable? In his 1990 article, "Format Integration: Handling Serials and Mixed Media," Stephen Davis gives an example of a "serially issued videodisc reproducing a map set, plus software to manipulate and display. The cataloging institution has decided to make the videorecording aspect primary; either the map or the computer file aspect might also have been made primary."[6] The resulting record has a visual materials 008 field, three 006 fields, one each for seriality, map aspects, and computer files, and two 007 fields, one for the video-recording and one for the map.

The above mentioned example is a theoretical one, selected to exemplify the full range of options available under Format Integration. But its very complexity raises an important question: Can libraries afford to do this level of coding? Those who originally designed the integrated format did not intend to impose more complexity on the cataloging process, particularly at a time when many institutions are struggling to maintain the same level of service with less staff. The designers' intent was to treat the *USMARC Format for Bibliographic Data* as a single data dictionary and to solve the seriality problem.

However, if libraries choose not to use this expanded coding, at least for special and rare materials, then nothing will have changed. The more flexible, powerful, informative online catalog envisioned after Format Integration will not be realized. Some of the note fields that previously were valid only for specific formats, but are now available for all materials, raise the same concerns. How and whether catalogers make use of the expanded capabilities of the integrated format are really matters of cataloging standards, to be decided within appropriate groups—utilities and their members, cataloging projects, and consortia. These mutual decisions will influence a host of other issues that are raised by the integrated formats, such as how input screens will look and what documentation will be needed.

Implementation

The greatest immediate impact falls upon system designers, both of local systems and of the bibliographic utilities. The utilities must take a lead in updating documentation and establishing usage standards, as well as modifying their systems to accept integrated records and use them. Local system designers also must be willing to make changes to support the integrated format. And support, in this case, does not simply mean permitting the input of a 006 field and adjusting validation tables. It also means, for example, including the 006 field in processes that previously depended on the Leader and the 008 field. If a system permits the user to limit searches by USMARC format, for example, then the first byte of the 006 field has to be included in the codes used to limit the search. Format integration implies that the problems caused by separate formats, such as multiple validation tables, display screens, and indexing routines, must be cured by changing well-established programs. The initial investment here may be very high.

Coordinating the implementation will be very complex since all record producers and receivers must be ready to accept and create integrated records at the same time. Phase 1 of the implementation was accomplished in late 1991, as the Library of Congress published the deleted elements and marked some others obsolete in USMARC format documentation. The utilities, for the most part, have implemented these changes, with the result that some libraries have had the opportunity to experience what happens when the system creating the record gets ahead of the system that receives it. Along with new record processing routines will come updated documentation—for example in the *USMARC Format for Bibliographic Data*, the utilities' versions of the format, editing guides, and the like. The major changes involved in Format Integration are being coordinated carefully among the Library of Congress, the bibliographic utilities, and local system vendors.

Beyond Format Integration

Having outlined what Format Integration will accomplish, I also must discuss some problems that appear to be format-related but that Format Integration does not resolve. For one thing, Format Integration does not solve what is really an acquisitions problem—how to set up a check-in record for a work that is issued as a series of monographs or that is updated by serially issued looseleaf updates. This is a design problem that probably should be addressed as part of a check-in system.

In her 1988 LITA presentation on Format Integration and the local catalog,

Karen Coyle listed four other such problems that bear attention:
- Although Format Integration allows us to create more complex records, it does not establish the "concept of a core record . . . a minimum record that unambiguously describes a bibliographic item." This kind of simplification also is necessary as we try to balance enhanced records against rising cataloging costs.
- Format Integration does not provide for "integration of local data." This appears to depend on wider acceptance of the USMARC Holdings Format. Until that happens, the multiple versions problem will not be resolved.
- The integrated format does not guarantee integrated access because there is no standard for index design, which leads to the next problem.
- Unresolved problems of integrating bibliographic and authority data remain. Questions on how authority and bibliographic index points should work together in the online catalog await further research and standards development before they can be answered satisfactorily.[7]

The need for system redesign and librarian training imposed by Format Integration undoubtedly will be expensive. For reference librarians there should be improvements, catalogers should see more continuity than change, and system designers can eventually expect an improved ability to meet customer needs. But the integrated format will make online catalogs more flexible and powerful if implemented properly, because it gives catalogers the opportunity to fully describe the material they catalog and users the opportunity to take advantage of that enriched description.

Notes

1. Library of Congress, Network Development and MARC Standards Office, *Format Integration and Its Effect on the USMARC Bibliographic Format*, 1992:5.
2. For a complete table of 006 field values, see Library of Congress, Network Development and MARC Standards Office, *Format Integration and Its Effect on the USMARC Bibliographic Format*, 1992:15-17.
3. Library of Congress, Network Development and MARC Standards Office, *Proposal no. 89-14: Changes to Leader/06 in the Bibliographic Format*, 1990:12.
4. Library of Congress, Network Development and MARC Standards Office, 1992.
5. The preceding three paragraphs were given in substantially the same form as part of the author's presentation "MARC Format Integration and Its Implications: The Librarian's Perspective" at the LITA Second National Conference, Boston, October 5, 1988.
6. Stephen P. Davis, "Format Integration: Handling Serials and Mixed Media," *Information Technology and Libraries* 9 (1990), 166.
7. Karen E. Coyle, "The Local Catalog Perspective," in *MARC Format Integration: Three Perspectives* (Chicago: American Library Association, 1990), 18-19.

Cataloging after Format Integration

Glenn Patton and Paul J. Weiss

Format Integration in Brief

The goal of Format Integration is the creation of a single USMARC bibliographic format that provides the complete range of content designation for all types of materials and in which all information of the same type is identified by the same content designation. Format Integration provides for the communication of records for complex items whose descriptions may include serial, archival control, and/or multiple material-type aspects.

Cataloging Problems before Format Integration

Changes in cataloging practices under Format Integration will not be as sweeping as some might expect. Most materials are already handled adequately in the current formats and will remain so after Format Integration. There are, however, some kinds of items, mainly multiformat items, that have posed problems in the current formats:

- Items with Accompanying Material of a Different Material Type
  for example, a computer file with a printed user's manual, a textbook with accompanying slides, a print journal with accompanying computer disk supplements

- Items Composed of Equally Predominant Portions That Are Different Types of Material

  for example, a kit made up of a videorecording, computer files, a sound cassette, and several maps; an archival collection containing books, photographs, manuscripts, and manuscript scores; a book containing text and scores
- Items That Are Simultaneously Multiple Types of Material

  for example, an atlas, a videorecording serial, an archival collection of posters, a looseleaf item that is updated monthly

Many of these kinds of materials did not exist (or did not exist in libraries) at the time of the development of the USMARC formats. In many cases, the growth of technology and the adoption of that technology have brought these materials into existence and into our collections—and into our lives as catalogers.

The basis of the problem in tagging such materials is that USMARC coding practice before Format Integration requires the cataloger to choose only one format for a record. This is coded in Leader byte 06 (Type of Record) and Leader byte 07 (Bibliographic Level) for the monograph/serial distinction. This selection of format then restricts which types of 007 and 008 fields can be used, as well as the choice of variable fields. Some information related to an item, thus, currently cannot be included in the USMARC record or will be tagged differently in different formats (e.g., 500 vs. a specific 5XX field). The only exception is kits, for the cataloger can use any type of 007 field that is relevant.

Most items involve only one type of material, so the choice is easy. In the case of a single-material item with accompanying material of a different type, the format of the main item is selected. For example, a word processing program with a user's manual is input into the Computer Files format, not the Books format.

Items composed of equally predominant portions that are different types of material have been dealt with by somewhat arbitrary, but consistent, decisions. It was decided to put kits in the Visual Materials format (even if there is no visual material in the kit). Mixed archival collections generally are handled in the AMC format. Books with text and music are divided into formats based on their subject classification.

Items that are simultaneously multiple types of material have proven to be the most problematic. Sometimes the choice of format is the result of agreements in cooperative programs: CONSER practices require that nonprint serials be entered in the Serials format. Sometimes it is more arbitrary: LC's Geography and Map Division considers, to paraphrase

Gertrude Stein, that "a map is a map is a map," regardless of its physical form. Other influences on the choice of format include limitations of particular systems and the organization of particular cataloging departments.

The requirement to make a format decision has inevitably caused disagreements about the "correct" format for a particular item. A shared database such as OCLC's Online Union Catalog contains multiple types of records for a single item because some users choose to treat the item in one way, while other users choose to treat it in a different way. OCLC staff sometimes have had to arbitrate "format wars" about nonprint serials.

Format Integration Solutions

One solution that Format Integration offers is the new 006 field, which allows the coding of additional fixed-length data elements. The field contains the material-specific "heart" of each of the existing 008 fields, with one additional character at the beginning to identify the type of material. Since the field is repeatable, it can be used to code data for multiple types of materials within a single bibliographic record, as well as multiple pieces of a single material-type item that have different characteristics. This field is optional; deciding when to use it will be a mix of local preference, consortium and utility policy, national consensus, and the characteristics of the item in hand.

Since any type of material may fall under archival control, Leader byte 08 (Type of Control) was defined as a way of separating this information from Leader byte 06. Value "a" indicates that the item is controlled archivally.

As another remedy, usage of field 007 is no longer restricted to particular Type of Record codes in Leader byte 06. Any type of 007 field now can be used in any bibliographic record (if it is relevant). This, in combination with the availability of field 006 and the extension of all existing 0XX fields (Numbers and Codes) for all types of materials, will ensure that catalogers can record all desired coded data for any item.

What this means is that the concept of the "format" of a record basically ceases to exist. It will be true that only a single Type of Record code can appear in Leader byte 06, and that this code, in combination with Leader byte 07 for books and serials, will dictate the type of 008 field in the record. However, any other Type of Record code and corresponding fixed-length data elements can appear in the record in 006 fields. The range of variable control fields (00X) and variable data fields (01X-9XX) no longer will be limited, and the tagging of a particular data element will be consistent for all materials.

The selection of a Type of Record code will be the same as it is now for most items. Items with a single material type will receive the code for that type, and items with accompanying material of a different type will be coded for the material type of the main item. Items composed of equally predominant parts that are different material types can be handled in the following manner: Kits still should be coded as kits (but catalogers are no longer locked into choosing visual materials fields), and new value "p" (Mixed Material) should be used for mixed archival collections. Items that are simultaneously more than one material type can be given any of the applicable codes.

Other Effects of Format Integration

Although the Leader, 006, 007, and 008 changes described above together constitute the most significant effect of Format Integration, there are others. Described below are the methods used in accomplishing the goal of Format Integration and their consequences.

Extended Data Elements

All data elements that are to be retained will be extended for use with all types of materials. This does not imply that all data elements actually will be used for all types of materials; rather, the extension of existing data elements allows the material itself (or, more accurately, the bibliographic description prepared for the item) to determine what content designation is appropriate instead of having the "format" determine what can be used.

Included among the extensions are the availability of material-specific and specialized note fields (5XX fields) for all types of materials. Examples include field 546 (Language Note), previously used in the Serials and AMC formats, which will be used for language information for all types of material, and field 521 (Target Audience Note), previously used in the AMC, Computer Files, Visual Materials, and Serials formats, which will be used for "intended audience" information for all materials (including, for example, children's books).

The extension of all linking fields (76X-78X) to all types of materials is important in describing serially issued materials of all types, while the capability to indicate that any kind of material is under archival control is facilitated by the extension of the archivally related subfields of fields 245 (Title Statement) and 300 (Physical Description) and of fields 541 (Immediate Source of Acquisition) and 584 (Accumulation and Frequency of Use).

These extensions, of course, created some conflicts because the same information appears in different places in the existing formats. These "overlaps" have been reconciled by establishing one place for the data and making the other fields obsolete. For example, before Format Integration, frequency information for serial publications appears in field 310 (Current Frequency) and field 321 (Former Frequency) in the Serials format and in field 315 (Frequency) in the Maps and Computer Files formats. After Format Integration, fields 310 and 321 will be used for frequency data for all material types and field 315 will be made obsolete. Another example of overlap is acquisitions data. This information (source, price, stock number, form of issue, etc.) has been recorded in fields 037 (Stock Number), 265 (Source for Acquisition/Subscription Address), and 350 (Price), depending on the type of material. In the future, field 037, renamed "Source of Acquisition," will be used for all such information, and fields 265 and 350 will be made obsolete.

The most noticeable of these overlaps may well be how varying forms of title have been recorded. In the Serials format, field 246 (Varying Form of Title) has been used for this information, while, in the other formats, field 740 (Added Entry—Variant Title) contains varying titles, as well as other kinds of title added entries. This conflict has been reconciled by using field 246 for all varying forms of title of the item. Field 740 has been renamed "Added Entry—Uncontrolled Related/Analytical Title," and its use is to be limited to titles of related works and works contained within the item that are not in heading form (i.e., those that normally would be entered under a name/title heading or whose heading form is not determined).

Data Elements Made Obsolete

Some elements, including some defined in the earliest years of MARC, have been identified as no longer useful (due, for example, to changes in computer technology or cataloging rules and practices) and are being made obsolete. Examples include field 008 byte 32 (Main Entry in Body of Entry), the second indicator in 1XX fields (Main Entry), both indicators in field 260 (Publication, Distribution, etc.), and some of the values used in the second indicator of fields 700-740 (Added Entry).

Added Data Elements

Some important new elements have been added to the integrated format, in addition to those mentioned already. Leader byte 06 (Type of Record) has an added code "t" for Manuscript Language Materials. A previously unused byte of the Leader, byte 08, has been defined as "Type of Control." Subfield ‡5 (Institution to Which Field Applies) has been added to eight 5XX fields. The value "blank (Undefined)" was added to a number of indicator positions. Some of these result from values that were made obsolete by Format Integration.

Deleted Data Elements and Name Changes

Two additional methods, deleted data elements and name changes, have less effect on day-to-day cataloging. Only eight elements were deleted; none had ever been used. Names generally were changed simply for clarification, such as the change to field 256 from File Characteristics to Computer File Characteristics.

Examples

This quick tour of the effects of Format Integration could not possibly cover all the details of how format changes affect the coding of various types of materials. To become more familiar with the changes, you may wish to spend some time with *Format Integration and Its Effect on the USMARC Format* (Washington, D.C.: Library of Congress, 1992). The examples in the following chapters, however, give some specific problems of USMARC coding practice before Format Integration and some solutions that Format Integration offers.

All of the example records represent real items. The records contain only those fields that are relevant to Format Integration and a basic bibliographic description. In these examples, the following conventions are followed:

* (in Leader) = system-supplied value

/ (in Leader, 006-008) = blank or fill character

$ = subfield delimiter

underlined text in "after" examples indicates areas of change in the record

Monographic Materials

Derry C. Juneja

The introduction of Format Integration will have less impact on monographic titles than on any other type of material discussed in this book. Most monographs represent printed material—that is, "a nonserial item, i.e., an item either complete in one part or complete, or intended to be completed, in a finite number of separate parts."[1]

Occasionally, however, an item appears that is obviously a monograph but that also contains some other medium. Some examples of mixed media that have posed problems include the following:

- Monograph with a Map
  Maps can be anything from one or more sheets inserted into a pocket to an atlas, which is itself described in the Books format. Maps also can take nonpaper forms, such as an inflatable globe.
- Monograph with Computer Disks
  Computer disks can be text files issued in conjunction with a monograph. In this case the monograph is not a user's manual. Instead, the disks supplement the text, rather than the text introducing or explaining the computer program.
- Monograph with Visual Items
  Monographs with visual items often are associated with juvenile material—for example, a book that comes with an accompanying item, such as a finger puppet.

Because of the rigidity of the USMARC formats, up to now there has been no method by which mixed media material could be identified. The USMARC format and coding practice have required choosing a single format for a record. Once the primary format is selected, the item is coded with the specific 008 field (Fixed-Length Data Elements) and with the variable fields available for that format. Because the 008 field is not repeatable, fixed-field information for other formats represented in the item cannot be coded. This means that once the primary format is chosen it is not always possible to reflect in coded form the important characteristics of accompanying items. Format Integration allows the coding of multiple material types in a single USMARC record.

One of the first things to do when cataloging multiple format materials is to select the primary format. In many cases the primary format is obvious. The examples shown in this chapter are all cases in which the primary format is a book, although other materials may be included in the item. The choice of primary format does not change when these books are recataloged under Format Integration. What does change is that data that previously were limited to sections of field 300 (Physical Description) now can be expressed in other variable fields and in the new 006 field (Fixed-Length Data Elements—Additional Material Characteristics).

The Leader in the USMARC format is still used to identify a Type of Record code. The USMARC Leader, in combination with an 008 field and one or more 006 fields, will ensure that any aspect of the item can be coded. Although multiple 006 fields and the 007 field (Physical Description Fixed Field) can be used to cover other aspects of the item, the examples given here contain only one 006 field. In addition to the fixed fields, any variable field that is appropriate to the cataloging of the item is available for use.

All of the following examples are considered to be primarily textual monographs; therefore, the Leader will be coded "a" for Language Material in the Type of Record code and "m" for Monograph in the Bibliographic Level code.

Note

1. *Anglo-American Cataloguing Rules, second edition. Revisions 1983,* Joint Steering Committee for Revision of AACR (Chicago: American Library Association, 1984), 568.

Example 1
Monograph with No Change

Example 1 is for a "normal" monograph, i.e., one that is strictly textual, with no variations in title. No decisions need to be made as to whether this is mixed media; clearly it is not. The only change in this record would be the omission of the second indicator in field 100 (Main Entry—Personal Name), a change that already has been implemented.

Example 1A
Monograph with No Change
Before Format Integration

```
LDR    *****nam//22*****/a/4500                              [Monograph]
008    760329s1971////nyu//////////000/1/eng//              [Monograph]

010         $a   71135186
100    10   $a Francis, Dick.
245    10   $a Rat race / $c Dick Francis.
250         $a 1st U.S. ed.
260         $a New York : $b Harper & Row, $c c1971.
300         $a 214 p. ; $c 22 cm.
490    0    $a A Harper novel of suspense
```

Example 1B
Monograph with No Change
After Format Integration

```
LDR    *****nam//22*****/a/4500                              [Monograph]
008    760329s1971////nyu//////////000/1/eng//              [Monograph]

010         $a   71135186
100    1_   $a Francis, Dick.
245    10   $a Rat race / $c Dick Francis.
250         $a 1st U.S. ed.
260         $a New York : $b Harper & Row, $c c1971.
300         $a 214 p. ; $c 22 cm.
490    0    $a A Harper novel of suspense
```

Example 2
Monograph with Computer Disks

Learn BASIC Now is accompanied by three computer disks. Example 2A shows how this is cataloged today. Example 2B uses the Leader and 008 field to indicate primary format (monograph) and then makes use of an 006 field to bring out features of the computer disk format, primarily the target audience and the type of computer file. Also note the use of field 516 (Type of Computer File or Data Note), previously used only for computer files and now available for use across all formats.

Example 2A
Monograph with Computer Disks
Before Format Integration

```
LDR   *****nam//22*****/a/4500                          [Monograph]
008   900123s1989////waua////////////001/0/eng//        [Monograph]

010        $a   89013234
100   1    $a Halvorson, Michael.
245   10   $a Learn BASIC now / $c Michael Halvorson & David Rygmyr ; foreword
           by Bill Gates.
260        $a Redmond, Wash. : $b Microsoft Press, $c c1989.
300        $a xvi, 490 p. : $b ill. ; $c 24 cm. + $e 3 computer disks (5 1/4
           in.)
500        $a System requirements for computer discs: IBM PC, PS/2, or
           compatible computer; at least 512KB; IBM CGA, EGA, or VGA, and
           compatible monitor (to take full advantage of color and graphics
           programs), or Hercules Graphics Card, or IBM MDA (runs all but a
           few programs); 1-2 disk drives or hard disk; printer and mouse
           supported.
700   10   $a Rygmyr, David, $d 1958-
```

Example 2B
Monograph with Computer Disks
After Format Integration

```
LDR   *****nam//22*****/a/4500                          [Monograph]
008   900123s1989////waua////////////001/0/eng//        [Monograph}
006   m////////d/////////                               [Computer Files]
```

```
010        $a    89013234
100   1    $a Halvorson, Michael.
245   10   $a Learn BASIC now / $c Michael Halvorson & David Rygmyr ; foreword
           by Bill Gates.
260        $a Redmond, Wash. : $b Microsoft Press, $c c1989.
300        $a xvi, 490 p. : $b ill. ; $c 24 cm. + $e 3 computer disks (5 1/4
           in.)
516        $a System requirements for computer discs: IBM PC, PS/2, or
           compatible computer; at least 512KB; IBM CGA, EGA, or VGA, and
           compatible monitor (to take full advantage of color and graphics
           programs), or Hercules Graphics Card, or IBM MDA (runs all but a
           few programs); 1-2 disk drives or hard disk; printer and mouse
           supported.
700   1    $a Rygmyr, David, $d 1958-
```

Example 3
Monograph with Single Map

This example is a monographic environmental impact report that contains a map in a pocket. The 006 field in Example 3B brings out the elements of the map, Type of Map, code "e," for printed map.

Example 3A
Monograph with Single Map
Before Format Integration

```
LDR   *****nam//22*****/a/4500                    [Monograph]
008   860129s1985////cauab/////////000/0/eng/d    [Monograph]

110   10  $a San Bernardino County (Calif.).  $b Housing and Community
          Development Dept.
245   10  $a Agua Mansa enterprise zone, final application, draft
          environmental impact report / $c prepared for County of San
          Bernardino, County of Riverside, [et al.] ; prepared by Wildan
          Associates.
260   0   $a Norwalk, Calif. : $b Wildan Associates, $c 1985.
300       $a 2 v. : $b ill., map ; $c 28 cm.
500       $a "November 1985."
500       $a One folded map in pocket.
504       $a Includes bibliography.
710   20  $a Wildan Associates (Norwalk, Calif.)
```

Example 3B
Monograph with Single Map
After Format Integration

```
LDR   *****nam//22*****/a/4500              [Monograph]
008   860129s1985////cauab/////////000/0/eng/d    [Monograph]
006   ei//////a/////0///                    [Map]
```

110	1	$a San Bernardino County (Calif.). $b Housing and Community Development Dept.
245	10	$a Agua Mansa enterprise zone, final application, draft environmental impact report / $c prepared for County of San Bernardino, County of Riverside, [et al.] ; prepared by Wildan Associates.
260		$a Norwalk, Calif. : $b Wildan Associates, $c 1985.
300		$a 2 v. : $b ill., map ; $c 28 cm.
500		$a "November 1985."
500		$a One folded map in pocket.
504		$a Includes bibliography.
710	2	$a Wildan Associates (Norwalk, Calif.)

Example 4
Monograph with Puppet

A series of Spanish children's books recently has been published, each with finger puppets. (In this example, the finger puppet is a blue spider made of felt.) Example 4A shows how this book is cataloged currently. Example 4B not only gives an 006 field but also indicates the differences between field 740 (Added Entry—Uncontrolled Related/Analytical Title) and field 246 (Varying Form of Title), which will be described later. The 006 field given is for visual materials, with the type code of "o" for kit. The target audience is listed as preschool, code "a."

Example 4A
Monograph with Puppet
Before Format Integration

```
LDR   *****nam//22*****/a/4500                    [Monograph]
008   910206s1991////caua///j//////000/1/spa/d   [Monograph]

010       $a   90062626
100  1    $a Cahill, Chris.
245  14   $a Una araña encantadora = $b Spider magic / $c [escrito por Chris
          Cahill; illustrado por Mitchell Rose ; traducido por Cecelia
          Ramires-Castro].
250       $a Ed. bilingüe.
260       $a San Francisco, CA : $b Schneider Educational Products, $c c1991.
300       $a 1 v. (unpaged) : $b col. ill. ; $c 15 cm. + $e 1 finger puppet.
440   0   $a Libro del dedo mágico
500       $a Translation of: Spider magic.
520       $a This play book includes a finger puppet spider to keep infants
          and young children entertained.
700  10   $a Rose, Mitchell.
740  01   $a Spider magic.
```

Example 4B
Monograph with Puppet
After Format Integration

```
LDR   *****nam//22*****/a/4500              [Monograph]
008   910206s1991////caua///j//////000/1/spa/d    [Monograph]
006   onnn/a///////////wn                   [Kit]

010       $a   90062626
100   1   $a Cahill, Chris.
245   14  $a Una araña encantadora = $b Spider magic / $c [escrito por Chris
          Cahill; illustrado por Mitchell Rose ; traducido por Cecelia
          Ramires-Castro].
246   11  $a Spider magic.
250       $a Ed. bilingüe.
260       $a San Francisco, CA : $b Schneider Educational Products, $c c1991.
300       $a 1 v. (unpaged) : $b col. ill. ; $c 15 cm. + $e 1 finger puppet.
440   0   $a Libro del dedo mágico
500       $a Translation of: Spider magic.
520       $a This play book includes a finger puppet spider to keep infants
          and young children entertained.
700   1   $a Rose, Mitchell.
```

Example 5
Monograph with Globe

Example 5 is a book accompanied by an inflatable globe. Example 5B shows how the additional 006 field for the globe, with a type code of "e" for printed map and "n" in the special format characteristics, identifies the globe.

Example 5A
Monograph with Globe
Before Format Integration

```
LDR   *****nam//22*****/a/4500              [Monograph]
008   911004s1991////nyu////j/b////000/0/eng//   [Monograph]

010       $a  91050382 /AC
100   1   $a Wolfman, Ira.
245   10  $a My world & globe / $c by Ira Wolfman ; with illustrations by
          Paul Meisel.
260       $a New York : $b Workman Pub., $c 1991.
300       $a 64 p. : $b ill. ; $c 20 cm + $e 1 inflatable globe.
490   0   $a An interactive first book of geography
520       $a Introduces the geography of the world. Includes an inflatable
          globe on which boundaries can be drawn, countries labeled, and
          stickers pasted.
700   1   $a Meisel, Paul.
```

Example 5B
Monograph with Globe
After Format Integration

```
LDR  *****nam//22*****/a/4500
008  911004s1991////nyu////j/b////000/0/eng//        [Monograph]
006  e///////d/////0/n/                               [Map]

010        $a  91050382 /AC
100  1     $a Wolfman, Ira.
245  10    $a My world & globe / $c by Ira Wolfman ; with illustrations by
           Paul Meisel.
260        $a New York : $b Workman Pub., $c 1991.
300        $a 64 p. : $b ill. ; $c 20 cm + $e 1 inflatable globe.
490        $a An interactive first book of geography
520        $a Introduces the geography of the world. Includes an inflatable
           globe on which boundaries can be drawn, countries labeled, and
           stickers pasted.
700  1     $a Meisel, Paul.
```

Example 6
Monograph as Atlas

Because atlases are books of maps, they are monographs. However, atlases also are considered to be maps. Format Integration provides the opportunity to code the map format information in the 006 field. Example 6 is a book of maps listed as an atlas in field 300. Example 6A shows current cataloging and Example 6B has the additional 006 field using code "e" for printed map and material type "b" to show that the item contains a series of maps.

Example 6A
Monograph as Atlas
Before Format Integration

```
LDR   *****nam//22/a/4500                        [Monograph]
008   841208s1984////nyub/////b////000/0/eng//   [Monograph]

010        $a   84675087/
100   10   $a Kidron, Michael.
245   14   $a The new state of the world atlas / $c Michael Kidron & Ronald
           Segal.
250        $a [2nd ed., rev.]
255        $a Scale not given.
260   0    $a New York : $b Simon & Schuster, $c c1984.
300        $a 1 atlas ([174] p.) : $b 57 col. maps ; $c 26 cm.
500        $a "Pluto Press project."
504        $a Includes bibliographies.
700   10   $a Segal, Ronald, $d 1932-
```

Example 6B
Monograph as Atlas
After Format Integration

```
LDR   *****nam//22/a/4500                          [Monograph]
008   841208s1984////nyub/////b////000/0/eng//     [Monograph]
006   e///////b/////0///                           [Map]


010        $a   84675087/ $o 10694681
100   1    $a Kidron, Michael.
245   14   $a The new state of the world atlas / $c Michael Kidron & Ronald
           Segal.
250        $a [2nd ed., rev.]
255        $a Scale not given.
260        $a New York : $b Simon & Schuster, $c c1984.
300        $a 1 atlas ([174] p.) : $b 57 col. maps ; $c 26 cm.
500        $a "Pluto Press project."
504        $a Includes bibliographies.
700   1    $a Segal, Ronald, $d 1932-
```

Example 7
Monograph with Analytical Titles

With Format Integration, one of the major changes affecting monographs is the use of field 246, which previously was assigned only to serials and computer files. Field 246 is to be used for titles other than those specifically provided for in fields 210-245. For books, etc., these formerly were carried in field 740. That field now will be limited to related-item titles and analytical titles.

Example 7 shows no changes except for those USMARC codes that already have been considered obsolete, such as the Main Entry in the Body of the Entry in the 008 field, and the omission of some indicators. Because the added entry titles are taken from the work, they are considered to be analytical and remain in field 740, as shown in Example 7B.

Example 7A
Monograph with Analytical Titles
Before Format Integration

```
LDR   *****nam//22*****///4500                    [Monograph]
008   761126s1974////nyu////////////000/1/eng//   [Monograph]

010      $a   740006554
100  10  $a Christie, Agatha, $d 1890-1976.
245  10  $a Murder on board; $b including The mystery of the Blue Train,
         What Mrs. McGillicuddy Saw! [and] Death in the air. $c [By]
         Agatha Christie.
260  0   $a New York, $b Dodd, Mead $c c1974.
300      $a 601 p. $c 22 cm.
740  01  $a Death in the air.
740  01  $a What Mrs. McGillicuddy saw!
740  41  $a The mystery of the Blue Train.
```

Example 7B
Monograph with Analytical Titles
After Format Integration

```
LDR    *****nam//22*****///4500                  [Monograph]
008    761126s1974////nyu/////////////000/1/eng//    [Monograph]
```

```
010        $a    740006554
100  1_    $a Christie, Agatha, $d 1890-1976.
245  10    $a Murder on board; $b including The mystery of the Blue Train,
           What Mrs. McGillicuddy saw! [and] Death in the air. $c [By] Agatha
           Christie.
260  __    $a New York, $b Dodd, Mead, $c c1974.
300        $a 601 p. $c 22 cm.
740  02    $a Death in the air.
740  02    $a What Mrs. McGillicuddy saw!
740  42    $a The mystery of the Blue Train.
```

Example 8
Monograph with Parallel Title

Example 8 contains a parallel title. This varying form of title formerly would have been coded in field 740, as shown in Example 8A, but it now is placed in field 246 as a varying form of title, as shown in Example 8B.

Example 8A
Monograph with Parallel Title
Before Format Integration

```
LDR   *****nam//22*****/a/4500                        [Monograph]
008   811209s1981////ohua//////////001/0/eng/d        [Monograph]

010        $a   80053395
245   00   $a Bilingual business grammar = $b gramática comercial bilingüe /
           $c Louis Chacon ... [et al.].
260   0    $a Cincinnati : $b South-Western, $c c1981.
300        $a xiii, 185 p. : $b ill. ; $c 25 cm.
650   0    $a Spanish language $x Business Spanish.
650   0    $a English language $x Business English.
700   10   $a Chacon, Louis.
740   00   $a Gramática comercial bilingüe.
```

Example 8B
Monograph with Parallel Title
After Format Integration

```
LDR   *****nam//22*****/a/4500                        [Monograph]
008   811209s1981////ohua//////////001/0/eng/d        [Monograph]

010        $a   80053395
245   00   $a Bilingual business grammar = $b gramática comercial bilingüe /
           $c Louis Chacon ... [et al.].
246   31   $a Gramática comercial bilingüe
260   __   $a Cincinnati : $b South-Western, $c c1981.
300        $a xiii, 185 p. : $b ill. ; $c 25 cm.
546        $a In English and Spanish.
650   0    $a Spanish language $x Business Spanish.
650   0    $a English language $x Business English.
700   1_   $a Chacon, Louis.
```

Example 9
Monograph with Varying Form of Title

Example 9 has a partial title, *Dictionary of Troublesome Words*. This needs to be emphasized as part of the title but is not a separate entity within the work. Previously coded in field 740, as shown in Example 9A, it is now coded in field 246, as shown in Example 9B.

Example 9A
Monograph with Varying Form of Title
Before Format Integration

```
LDR   *****nam//22*****/a/4500                    [Monograph]
008   860107s1985////nyu///////bd///000/0/eng//   [Monograph]

010        $a   87033046
100   10   $a Bryson, Bill.
245   14   $a The Facts on File dictionary of troublesome words / $c Bill
           Bryson.
250        $a Rev. ed.
260   0    $a New York, N.Y. : $b Facts on File, $c c1987.
300        $a 192 p. ; $c 24 cm.
504        $a Bibliography: p. 186-187.
650   0    $a English language $x Usage $x Dictionaries.
650   0    $a English language $x Rhetoric.
710   20   $a Facts on File, Inc.
740   01   $a Dictionary of troublesome words.
```

Example 9B
Monograph with Varying Form of Title
After Format Integration

```
LDR   *****nam//22*****/a/4500                    [Monograph]
008   860107s1985////nyu///////bd///000/0/eng//   [Monograph]

010        $a   87033046
100  1     $a Bryson, Bill.
245  14    $a The Facts on File dictionary of troublesome words / $c Bill
           Bryson.
246  10    $a Dictionary of troublesome words.
250        $a Rev. ed.
260        $a New York, N.Y. : $b Facts on File, $c c1987.
300        $a 192 p. ; $c 24 cm.
504        $a Bibliography: p. 186-187.
650   0    $a English language $x Usage $x Dictionaries.
650   0    $a English language $x Rhetoric.
710   2    $a Facts on File, Inc.
```

Multimedia Materials

Glenn Patton

Format Integration will be particularly useful for cataloging mixed-media items. Some of the hard-to-catalog items have grown out of technology introduced since the original development of the USMARC formats. Other items are the result of new options for reproducing or preserving materials.

Some classic examples of mixed media that have posed problems in the current formats include the following:

- a map that is a puzzle
- a computer file that is a game
- a computer file with a user's manual
- a kit containing a videorecording, computer files, a sound cassette, and several maps
- microscope slides reproduced on videodisc

The problem for each of these mixed-media examples is that current USMARC structure and coding practice require that the cataloger choose only one format for a record. One then is locked into that format for coded values in the 008 field and for the selection of variable fields available in that format. The only exception is in coding for kits. Since any of the existing types of 007 fields was valid for that format type, at least some aspects of the formats can be coded.

Because the Type of Record code in the Leader and the 008 field are linked closely together, and because the 008 field is not repeatable, choosing the primary format usually also means that one cannot code any other characteristics, no matter how important those characteristics might be.

Under Format Integration, however, the new, repeatable 006 field lets one code multiple kinds of materials within a single bibliographic record. In addition, field 007 now can be used with any format type. Together, these fields will ensure that one can code any aspect of a mixed-media item. Although one still will need to choose a primary format, this task for multimedia materials should be simpler, thanks to the model laid out in *Format Integration and Its Effect on the USMARC Bibliographic Format* This model should become a prominent part of USMARC documentation as well as the bibliographic utility's documentation:

> If an item is basically textual, then the primary format will be coded for Language Material (Type of Material: a), Manuscript Language Material (Type of Material: t), or Mixed Material (Type of Material: p). The 008 field would be coded for book, serials, or archival and manuscript control.

> If an item is *not* basically textual, then the primary format will be chosen from among one of the Type of Material codes appropriate for music, maps, sound recordings, computer files, or visual materials, and the matching 008 field will be used.[1]

One must keep in mind that, in the second case, the general AACR2 rule (rule 0.24) points to the physical form of the item in hand as the starting point of the cataloging process.[2] Multiple 006 and 007 fields then can be used to cover any other aspects of the item. In addition, any variable field that is appropriate to the form or control of the item is available for use.

Example 1
Computer File with an Accompanying Book

Example 1 is a common example of an item that combines multiple characteristics. Most computer files have some kind of accompanying material, and many kinds of AV materials have a user's guide. Choosing to use an 006 field to describe the accompanying material is open to question, especially if it is only a small booklet. In this case, the user's manual is substantial and has many illustrations; therefore, I have included an 006 field reflecting this. Without this field, the record would look much as it would have before Format Integration.

Example 1A
Computer File with an Accompanying Book Before Format Integration

```
LDR   *****nmm//22*****/a/4500              [computer file]
008   920511s1992////ctun///e///m////////////d    [computer file]

100  1     $a Tobias, Andrew P.
240  10    $a Managing your money
245  10    $a Andrew Tobias' managing your money $h [computer file].
250        $a IBM version 8.0.
256        $a Computer data and programs.
260        $a Fairfield, CT : $b MECA Software, $c 1992.
300        $a 4 computer disks ; $c 5 1/4 in. + $e 1 user's guide (320
           p. : ill. ; 23 cm.)
```

Example 1B
Computer File with an Accompanying Book After Format Integration

```
LDR   *****nmm//22*****/a/4500              [computer file]
008   920511s1992////ctun///e///m////////////d    [computer file]
006   aa//////////001/0/                    [book]

100  1     $a Tobias, Andrew P.
240  10    $a Managing your money
245  10    $a Andrew Tobias' managing your money $h [computer file].
250        $a IBM version 8.0.
256        $a Computer data and programs.
260        $a Fairfield, CT : $b MECA Software, $c 1992.
300        $a 4 computer disks ; $c 5 1/4 in. + $e 1 user's guide (320
           p. : ill. ; 23 cm.)
```

Example 2
Map That Is a Puzzle

Example 2 is a classic example of mixed characteristics: a historic map used
as the basis of a jigsaw puzzle. Before Format Integration, the cataloger
would have chosen a primary format ("map" under LC's cataloging practice;
"three-dimensional artifact" if the puzzle aspect seemed primary), and the
other characteristics would have been lost. Choosing "map" would permit the
cataloger to deal with aspects of scale and coordinates, but the item could not
also be coded as a "game." Choosing "game" as the primary format would
have prevented the inclusion of scale and coordinates. Format Integration
allows the coding of all this information in a single USMARC record. The
cataloger can properly call it a game and code the Type of Record and field
008 for that, but also can include fields 006 and 007 to reflect the fact that the
jigsaw puzzle is also a map. Note that fields 034 (Coded Mathematical Data)
and 255 (Mathematical Data) also can be included. Field 246 (Varying Form
of Title) is used to trace the "other title information"; this replaces the use of
field 740 (Added Entry—Variant Title).

Example 2A
Map That Is a Puzzle
Before Format Integration (cataloged as a puzzle)

```
LDR   *****nrm//22*****/a/4500                        [game]
008   831021r19811579enknnn/g//////////0gneng/d      [game]

100  1    $a Terwoort, Lenaert.
245  10   $a Christopher Saxton's map of Cornwall $h [game] : $b first
          published 1579 : a hand cut wooden jigsaw puzzle :
          Promontorivm hoc in mare proiectvm Cornuvia dicitvr.
260       $a London : $b Optimago Ltd., $c [1981?]
300       $a 1 jigsaw puzzle (ca. 575 pieces) : $b wood, col. ; $c ca.
          44 x 56cm., in drawstring cotton bag, in box 32 x 23 x 6 cm.
740  01   $a Promontorivm hoc in mare proiectvm Cornuvia dicitvr.
```

Example 2B
Map That Is a Puzzle
Before Format Integration (cataloged as a map)

```
LDR   *****nem//22*****/a/4500                        [map]
007   az|cbfzn                                        [map]
008   831021r19811579enki//////a/////0///eng/d        [map]


100 1    $a Terwoort, Lenaert.
245 10   $a Christopher Saxton's map of Cornwall $h [game] : $b first
         published 1579 : a hand cut wooden jigsaw puzzle :
         Promontorivm hoc in mare proiectvm Cornuvia dicitvr.
255      $a Scale not given.
260      $a London : $b Optimago Ltd., $c [1981?]
300      $a 1 jigsaw puzzle (ca. 575 pieces) : $b wood, col. ; $c ca.
         44 x 56 cm., in drawstring cotton bag, in box 32 x 23 x 6 cm.
740 01   $a Promontorivm hoc in mare proiectvm Cornuvia dicitvr.
```

Example 2C
Map That Is a Puzzle
After Format Integration

```
LDR   *****nrm//22*****/a/4500                        [game]
007   az|cbfzn                                        [map]
008   831021r19811579enknnn/g///////////gneng/d       [game]
006   ei//////a/////0/1/                              [map]


100 1    $a Terwoort, Lenaert.
245 10   $a Christopher Saxton's map of Cornwall $h [game] : $b first
         published 1579 : a hand cut wooden jigsaw puzzle :
         Promontorivm hoc in mare proiectvm Cornuvia dicitvr.
246 30   $a Promontorivm hoc in mare proiectvm Cornuvia dicitvr
255      $a Scale not given.
260      $a London : $b Optimago Ltd., $c [1981?]
300      $a 1 jigsaw puzzle (ca. 575 pieces) : $b wood, col. ; $c ca.
         44 x 56 cm., in drawstring cotton bag, in box 32 x 23 x 6
         cm.
```

Example 3
Computer File That Is Also a Map

Example 3 is of a computer file that represents a map. The obvious primary format is "computer files" since that is its physical form, but the 006 field can be used to represent the fact that this is also a map. No 007 field was included because that field is not used for computer files and the map version is so oriented toward printed maps that there seemed to be no reasonable way to code it.

Example 3A
Computer File That Is Also a Map
Before Format Integration

```
LDR  *****nmm//22*****/a/4500              [computer file]
008  910719s1991////vaun///f///m/f//////eng/d    [computer file]
007  aj//znzn

100  1    $a Baskerville, Charles A.
245  10   $a Vermont landslide map $h [computer file]
          : $b a digital data set for IBM PC and compatible
          microcomputers / $c by Charles A. Baskerville.
250       $a Digital version.
256       $a Computer data and programs (30 files).
260       $a Reston, VA : $b U.S. Geological Survey ; $a Denver, Colo.
          : $b Books and Open-File Services Section [distributor], $c
          1991.
300       $a 5 computer disks ; $c 5 1/4 in. + $e 1 booklet (4 leaves
          ; 28 cm.)
```

Example 3B
Computer File That Is Also a Map
After Format Integration

```
LDR  *****nmm//22*****/a/4500                    [computer file]
008  910719s1991////vaun///f///m/f//////eng/d    [computer file]
006  e///////a//f//0/z/                          [map]
007  aj//znzn
```

```
100  1    $a Baskerville, Charles A.
245  10   $a Vermont landslide map $h [computer file]
          : $b a digital data set for IBM PC and compatible
          microcomputers / $c by Charles A. Baskerville.
250       $a Digital version.
255       $a Scale not given.
256       $a Computer data and programs (30 files).
260       $a Reston, VA : $b U.S. Geological Survey ; $a Denver, Colo.
          : $b Books and Open-File Services Section [distributor], $c
          1991.
300       $a 5 computer disks ; $c 5 1/4 in. + $e 1 booklet (4 leaves
          ; 28 cm.)
```

Example 4
Videodisc Combining Still and Moving Images

This videodisc is an example of a common combination of still and moving images on a single disc. As can be seen from the contents note, the disc includes more than 2,000 photographs of blood, marrow, and tissue samples; almost 2,000 more microscope slides of various kinds of physical abnormalities; 1,700 photographs of tumors; two short instructional films on red cell shapes and drawing blood; and a few nature photos thrown in for good measure. Prior to Format Integration, the cataloger could have coded this as a "videodisc" but would have had no way (other than in the contents note or a summary note) to indicate that all these still images were included.

Example 4A
Videodisc Combining Still and Moving Images
Before Format Integration

```
LDR   *****ngm//22*****/a/4500                    [videodisc]
007   vd|cgaizu                                   [videodisc]
007   kh|cuu                                      [photograph]
008   820211s1981////ctu023/fz/////////vleng/d    [videodisc]

245   00   $a Medical applications videodisc, hematology $h
           [videorecording] / $c Miles Learning Center.
260        $a West Haven, Conn. : $b Miles Pharmaceuticals, $c 1981.
300        $a 1 videodisc : $b sd., col. ; $c 12 in.
505   0    $a American Society of Hematology slide bank [photographs]
           (2080 fr.) — Western Universities physical diagnosis slide
           bank [microscope slides] (1912 fr.) — World Health
           Organization international histological classification of
           tumors [photographs] (1700 fr.) — Flora and fauna of
           Washington [photographs] (175 fr.) — Red cell shapes in
           disease (17 min.) — Venipuncture : the vacutainer system (6
           min.)
```

Example 4B
Videodisc Combining Still and Moving Images
After Format Integration

```
LDR    *****ngm//22*****/a/4500                    [videodisc]
007    vd|cgaizu                                   [videodisc]
007    kh|cuu                                      [photograph]
008    820211s1981////ctu023/fz/////////vleng/d    [videodisc]
006    rnnn/f//////////pn                          [microscope slide]
006    knnn/g//////////in                          [photograph]
```

```
245  00   $a Medical applications videodisc, hematology $h
          [videorecording] / $c Miles Learning Center.
260       $a West Haven, Conn. : $b Miles Pharmaceuticals, $c 1981.
300       $a 1 videodisc : $b sd., col. ; $c 12 in.
505  0    $a American Society of Hematology slide bank [photographs]
          (2080 fr.) — Western Universities physical diagnosis slide
          bank [microscope slides] (1912 fr.) — World Health
          Organization international histological classification of
          tumors [photographs] (1700 fr.) — Flora and fauna of
          Washington [photographs] (175 fr.) — Red cell shapes in
          disease (17 min.) — Venipuncture : the vacutainer system (6
          min.)
```

Example 5
Kit with Several Different Media

Example 5 is a classic kit: a set of filmstrips with accompanying sound on a cassette, several books, a poster, and three games. It still is coded as a kit, with 007 fields for the filmstrips and the poster; however, field 006 can be used to indicate the presence of the books and the games, which could not have been coded in the past.

Example 5A
Kit with Several Different Media
Before Format Integration

```
LDR   *****nom//22*****/a/4500                      [kit]
007   gf|cjbff/                                     [filmstrip]
007   ki|co/                                        [poster]
008   801111s1975////nyunnn/c//////////bneng/d      [kit]


245   00   $a Free to be — you and me multimedia module $h [kit].
260        $a New York : $b McGraw-Hill Film, $c 1975.
300        $a 6 filmstrips, 1 sound cassette, 1 guide book, 1 book, 1
           poster, 3 games ; $c in container, 30 x 23 x 6 cm.
```

Example 5B
Kit with Several Different Media
After Format Integration

```
LDR   *****nom//22*****/a/4500                      [kit]
007   gf|cjbff/                                     [filmstrip]
007   ki|co/                                        [poster]
008   801111s1975////nyunnn/c//////////bneng/d      [kit]
006   gnnn/c//////////fn                            [filmstrip]
006   aa///j//////000/0/                            [book]
006   knnn/c//////////in                            [poster]
006   rnnn/c//////////gn                            [game]


245   00   $a Free to be — you and me multimedia module $h [kit].
260        $a New York : $b McGraw-Hill Film, $c 1975.
300        $a 6 filmstrips, 1 sound cassette, 1 guide book, 1 book, 1
           poster, 3 games ; $c in container, 30 x 23 x 6 cm.
```

Example 6
Archival Collection Containing Multiple Media

Finally, here is an example of another kind of mixed collection: an archival collection that contains the "records" of a conference—all the papers that reflect the arrangements and funding for the conference plus the proceedings of the conference in various physical forms. The description has been prepared according to the Hensen APPM manual.[3] This previously would have been in the AMC format (Type of Record "b"). For this type of archival collection, the new "mixed material" type (Type of Record "p") is appropriate. The fact that the collection is under archival control is reflected by the code "a" in byte 8 of the Leader of the record. The 006 and 007 fields give details about the various media contained in the collection, including a Books 006 field beginning with code "t" to represent the "manuscript language material" that is present.

Example 6A
Archival Collection Containing Multiple Media
Before Format Integration

```
LDR   *****nbc//22*****/a/4500                    [AMC]
008   870417i19591983cau//////////////////eng/d    [AMC]

111  2    $a History of Programming Languages Conference $d (1978 : $c
          Los Angeles, Calif.)
245  00   $k Records, $f 1959, 1972-1983 $g (bulk 1976-1982).
300       $a7 $f cubic ft.
520  8    $a Correspondence, reports, draft presentations, newspaper
          clippings, notes, memoranda, National Science Foundation
          grant records, publicity materials, and mailing lists
          relating to the planning and organization of the conference.
          Also includes conference proceedings in the form of black-
          and-white video cassettes, reel-to-reel and cassette audio
          recordings, black-and-white photographs, slides, transcripts
          of presentations, preprints of papers, and book drafts. . . .
```

Example 6B
Archival Collection Containing Multiple Media
After Format Integration

```
LDR   *****npca/22*****/a/4500              [mixed material]
007   vf|bbahou                            [videorecording]
007   st|munumuunnuu                       [sound reel tape]
007   ss|lunjluunnuu                       [sound cassette]
007   kh|bou                               [photograph]
007   gs|uk//jc                            [slide]
008   870417i19591983cau/////////////////eng/d   [AMC]
006   g---/g//////////vl                   [videorecording]
006   innnnn///////c////                   [sound recording]
006   knnn/g//////////in                   [photograph]
006   gnnn/g//////////sn                   [slide]
006   t///////////10//0/                   [manuscript language material]
```

```
111   2     $a History of Programming Languages Conference $d (1978 : $c
            Los Angeles, Calif.)
245   00    $k Records, $f 1959, 1972-1983 $g (bulk 1976-1982).
300         $a7 $f cubic ft.
520   8     $a Correspondence, reports, draft presentations, newspaper
            clippings, notes, memoranda, National Science Foundation
            grant records, publicity materials, and mailing lists
            relating to the planning and organization of the conference.
            Also includes conference proceedings in the form of black-
            and-white video cassettes, reel-to-reel and cassette audio
            recordings, black-and-white photographs, slides, transcripts
            of presentations, preprints of papers, and book drafts. . . .
```

Notes

1. *Format Integration and Its Effect on the USMARC Bibliographic Format* (Washington, D.C.: Library of Congress, 1992), 9.
2. *Anglo-American Cataloguing Rules*, 2d ed., 1988 revision (Chicago: American Library Association, 1988), 8.
3. Steven L. Hensen, *Archives, Personal Papers, and Manuscripts,* 2d ed. (Chicago: Society of American Archivists, 1989).

Serials

Paul J. Weiss

Serials as a whole will probably be little affected by Format Integration. In the few cases in which data would have been assigned different content designation in the Serials format vs. other formats, the method defined in the USMARC Serials format was generally the one chosen. For example, varying titles for all material types will be tagged 246 (Varying Form of Title) after Format Integration rather than 740 (Added Entry—Variant Title). Among the types of publication codes in field 008 byte 06 (Fixed-Length Data Elements, Type of Publication Status), codes "c" and "d" retain their serial meanings (but with their names clarified as Serial Item Currently Published and Serial Item Ceased Publication); the monographic meanings were reassigned to new codes "t" and "e" (Publication Date and Copyright Date, and Detailed Date). Serial conventions for unknown and inapplicable portions of dates in field 008 bytes 07-14 were extended to the other types of material.

Some content designation that is used primarily in the Serials format is being made obsolete:

008 bytes 30-32 (Title Page Availability, Index Availability, and Cumulative Index Availability—changes already made)

212 (Variant Access Title)

265 (Source for Acquisition/Subscription Address)

512 (Earlier or Later Volumes Cataloged Separately)

570 (Editor)

Data formerly entered in field 265 will go into the renamed field 037 (Source of Acquisition); field 212 data will be added to field 246; and fields 512 and 570 information will go in field 500 (General Notes). Several indicators already have been made obsolete: field 222 (Key Title) indicator 1; field 260 (Publication, Distribution, etc.) indicators 1 and 2; and the 1XX fields (Main Entry) indicator 2. There are several new Note fields for serials that catalogers might find useful: field 501 (With Note), field 505 (Formatted Contents), field 522 (Geographic Coverage), field 524 (Preferred Citation of Described Materials), and field 540 (Terms Governing Use and Reproduction).

The biggest change for serials will be for nonprint serials. Instead of having to choose between the Serials format and the Computer Files, Maps, Visual Materials, or Music format, the cataloger will be able to code all applicable fixed-length data elements and use any appropriate variable fields. The Type of Record in the Leader is still only one byte long (byte 06), so only one code may be used there. For the sake of consistency across institutions and records, it was decided that nonprint serials should be coded for the nonprint aspect in Leader byte 06 and the corresponding 008 field. The serial aspect and any additional aspects will be coded in the 006 field (Fixed-Length Data Elements—Additional Material Characteristics), whose first byte indicates the type of material described in the 006 field.

For serials with supplements, the supplement now can be represented by its own Fixed-Length Data Element field (006 field). For serial supplements, most often the only difference between the main 008 field and the supplement's Serial 006 field will be the Frequency, but Regularity, Nature of Entire Work, Nature of Contents, Conference Publication, and other elements also may differ. For monographic supplements, a Books 006 field can be used to show Nature of Contents, Festschrift, or other elements. If the supplement is nonprint, a Visual Materials, Maps, Music, or Computer Files 006 field also can be used.

Example 1
Print Serial

Example 1 is a run-of-the-mill print serial. There are few changes. Note that this is a pre-AACR2 record; Format Integration affects records created under all versions of cataloging rules the same way. Although not present in this example, Serial note fields 512 (Earlier or Later Volumes Cataloged Separately) and 570 (Editor) are obsolete. Additional note fields now available that serial catalogers might find useful include field 501 (With Note), field 505 (Formatted Contents Note), field 522 (Geographic Coverage Note), field 524 (Preferred Citation of Described Materials Note), and field 540 (Terms Governing Use and Reproduction Note).

Example 1A
Print Serial
Before Format Integration

```
LDR         *****cas//22*****///4500                      [serials]
008         741011c19709999dcumn1pe//////0uuua0eng/d      [serials]

010         $a sn 78001596
022   0     $a 0030-0071
222   00    $a Off our backs
245   00    $a Off our backs.
260   00    $a Washington, $b Off Our Backs, inc.
265         $a Off Our Backs, 2423 18th St NW 2nd Floor, Washington, DC
            20009-2003
300         $a v. $b illus. $c 38-41 cm.
310         $a Monthly (except combined Aug./Sept. issue), $b <Oct. 1981->
321         $a Monthly, $b 1970-
350         $a $30.00
362   0     $a v. 1-   Feb. 1970-
```

Example 1B
Print Serial
After Format Integration

```
LDR        *****cas//22*****///4500              [serials]
008        741011c19709999dcumn1pe//////0///a0eng/d    [serials]

010        $a sn 78001596
022   0    $a 0030-0071
037        $b Off Our Backs, 2423 18th St NW 2nd Floor, Washington, DC
           20009-2003 $c $30.00
222   0    $a Off our backs
245   00   $a Off our backs.
260        $a Washington, $b Off Our Backs, inc.
300        $a v. $b illus. $c 38-41 cm.
310        $a Monthly (except combined Aug./Sept. issue), $b <Oct. 1981->
321        $a Monthly, $b 1970-
362   0    $a v. 1-   Feb. 1970-
```

Example 2
Musical Sound Recording Serial

This is an example of a nonprint serial. The primary changes here are the combination of data and specific content designation from the two formats that the item could have been entered in before. In addition to repeating 007 fields (Physical Description Fixed Field) when there are multiple formats involved, the 007 field can be repeated when a particular characteristic changes within the item. For example, when the Capture and Storage Technique changes from analog to digital, a new 007 field can be added.

Example 2A
Musical Sound Recording Serial Before Format Integration (cataloged in the Serials format)

```
LDR       *****cas//22*****/a/4500                [serials]
008       892507c19869999cauar//////////0uuua0eng/d    [serials]

245   00  $a From the pages of Experimental musical instruments $h [sound
          recording].
260   00  $a Nicasio, CA : $b Experimental Musical Instruments, $c 1986-
300       $a sound cassettes : $b analog, Dolby processed +
          $e    data sheets.
310       $a Annual
362   0   $a Vol. 1 (1986)-
520   8   $a Music of instruments that have appeared in Experimental
          musical instruments, a newsletter for the design, construction,
          and enjoyment of new sound sources.
710   20  $a Experimental Musical Instruments (Firm)
772   0   $t Experimental musical instruments $x 0883-0754 $w (DLC)sn
          85007492
```

Example 2B
Musical Sound Recording Serial Before Format Integration (cataloged in the Music format)

```
LDR          *****cjs//22*****/a/4500                    [music]
[or (depending on system restrictions)]
LDR          *****cjm//22*****/a/4500]                   [music]

007          ss|lunjlumnnce                              [sound cassette]
008          892507m19869999caufmn///fg//////0//////d   [music]
041    0     $g eng
```

```
245    00    $a From the pages of Experimental musical instruments $h [sound
             recording].
260    0     $a Nicasio, CA : $b Experimental Musical Instruments, $c 1986-
300          $a sound cassettes : $b analog, Dolby processed + $e    data
             sheets.
500          $a Annual; v. 1 (1986)-
520    8     $a Music of instruments that have appeared in Experimental
             musical instruments, a newsletter for the design, construction,
             and enjoyment of new sound sources.
580          $a Supplement to: Experimental musical instruments.
710    2     $a Experimental Musical Instruments (Firm)
```

Example 2C
Musical Sound Recording Serial After Format Integration

```
LDR          *****cjs//22*****/a/4500                    [music]
007          ss|lunjlumnnce                              [sound cassette]
008          892507m19869999caufmn///fg/////////////d   [music]
006          sar/////////0///a0                          [serial]
```

```
041    0     $g eng
245    00    $a From the pages of Experimental musical instruments $h [sound
             recording].
260          $a Nicasio, CA : $b Experimental Musical Instruments, $c 1986-
300          $a sound cassettes : $b analog, Dolby processed + $e    data
             sheets.
310          $a Annual
362    0     $a Vol. 1 (1986)-
520    8     $a Music of instruments that have appeared in Experimental
             musical instruments, a newsletter for the design, construction,
             and enjoyment of new sound sources.
710    2     $a Experimental Musical Instruments (Firm)
772    0     $t Experimental musical instruments $x 0883-0754 $w (DLC)sn
             85007492
```

Example 3
Monograph Accompanied by Serial Updates
That Are Not Cataloged Separately

The situation depicted in Example 3 happens infrequently now because serial updates generally are cataloged separately, but it does happen. Note that fields 310 (Current Publication Frequency) and 362 (Dates of Publication and/or Volume Designation) are still for the item as a whole and, therefore, are not appropriate for describing accompanying material. Field 547 (Former Title Complexity Note) is to be used only for the item in hand (possible for a multipart monograph, but not for different editions). Both fields 5XX could be 580 fields (Linking Entry Complexity Note). The usage of linking fields in monographic records after Format Integration was discussed by MARBI at the 1991 ALA Midwinter Meeting, but no consensus was reached.

Example 3A
Monograph Accompanied by Serial Updates
That Are Not Cataloged Separately
Before Format Integration

```
LDR         *****aam//22*****/a/4500                    [monograph]
008         900830s1990////paua/////bf///00100/eng//    [monograph]

010         $a    90063102
100   10    $a Hansten, Philip D.
245   10    $a Drug interactions & updates / $c Philip D. Hansten, John R.
            Horn.
260   0     $a Malvern, Pa. : $b Lea & Febiger ; $a Vancouver, Wash. : $b
            Applied Therapeutics, $c c1990.
300         $a 1 v. : $b ill. ; $c 30 cm.
500         $a New ed. published every other year; previous eds. entitled:
            Drug interactions.
500         $a Includes quarterly updates: Drug interactions newsletter &
            updates. Vol. 11, no. 1 (Jan. 1991)-
```

Example 3B
Monograph Accompanied by Serial Updates
That Are Not Cataloged Separately
After Format Integration

LDR		*****aam//22*****/a/4500	[monograph]
008		900830s1990////paua/////bf///001_0eng/	[monograph]
006		sqr/////////0////0	

010		$a 90063102
100	1	$a Hansten, Philip D.
245	10	$a Drug interactions & updates / $c Philip D. Hansten, John R. Horn.
260		$a Malvern, Pa. : $b Lea & Febiger ; $a Vancouver, Wash. : $b Applied Therapeutics, $c c1990.
300		$a 1 v. : $b ill. ; $c 30 cm.
500		$a New ed. published every other year; previous eds. entitled: Drug interactions.
525		$a Includes quarterly updates: Drug interactions newsletter & updates. Vol. 11, no. 1 (Jan. 1991)-
740	02	$a Drug interactions newsletter & updates.

Example 4
Serial Accompanied by Serial Updates
That Are Not Cataloged Separately

Example 4 is similar to Example 3 except that the main item itself is a serial. Only one byte of the 006 field differs from the 008 field; the cataloger might decide not to record it. Field 020 (ISBN) is, of course, optional. The cataloger also can decide not to record any 006 field. The change from the coding of the title from field 212 to field 246 does not necessitate the addition of an 006 field.

Example 4A
Serial Accompanied by Serial Updates
That Are Not Cataloged Separately
Before Format Integration

```
LDR        *****cas//22*****/a/4500                    [serial]
008        890523c19899999mduar/////////0uuu/0eng/d    [serial]

010        $a sn 89044162
022        $y 8756-6028
212   0    $a American hospital formulary service drug information
245   00   $a AHFS drug information.
260   00   $a Bethesda, MD : $b Published by authority of the Board of
           Directors of American Society of Hospital Pharmacists, $c c1989-
300        $a v. : $b ill. ; $c 28 cm.
310        $a Annual
362   0    $a 89-
525        $a Kept up to date by quarterly supplements.
780   00   $t American hospital formulary service drug information $x
           8756-6028 $w (DLC)    85644858 $w (OCoLC)10417225
```

Example 4B
Serial Accompanied by Serial Updates
That Are Not Cataloged Separately
After Format Integration

LDR		*****cas//22*****/a/4500	[serial]
008		890523c19899999mduar/////////0///0/0eng/d	[serial]
006		sqr//////////0////0	[serial]

010		$a sn 89044162
020		$a 1879907070 (1992)
022		$y 8756-6028
245	00	$a AHFS drug information.
246	20	$a American hospital formulary service drug information
260		$a Bethesda, MD : $b Published by authority of the Board of Directors of American Society of Hospital Pharmacists, $c c1989-
300		$a v. : $b ill. ; $c 28 cm.
310		$a Annual
362	0	$a 89-
525		$a Kept up to date by quarterly supplements.
780	00	$t American hospital formulary service drug information $x 8756-6028 $w (DLC) 85644858 $w (OCoLC)10417225

Example 5
Item That Is Looseleaf for Updating

This example shows the common situation of a base looseleaf volume that is updated (in this case irregularly). The primary change is the addition of a Serial 006 field, which may be useful in some local systems. For example, a draft check-in screen may be created based on the data in the 006 field.

Example 5A
Item That Is Looseleaf for Updating Before Format Integration

```
LDR        *****cam//22*****/a/4500              [monograph]
007        td                                    [text in loose-leaf
                                                  binder]
008        880204m19889999dcu//////b///f00100/eng//   [monograph]

010        $a    87600486 //r88
020        $a 0844405957 (loose-leaf)
245   00   $a USMARC format for bibliographic data : $b including guidelines
           for content designation / $c prepared by Network Development and
           MARC Standards Office.
260   0    $a Washington : $b Cataloging Distribution Service, Library of
           Congress, $c 1988-
300        $a 2 v. (loose-leaf) ; $c 28 cm.
```

Example 5B
Item That Is Looseleaf for Updating After Format Integration

```
LDR        *****cam//22*****/a/4500              [monograph]
007        td                                    [text in loose-leaf
                                                  binder]
008        880204m19889999dcu//////b///f001/0/eng//   [monograph]
006        s/x/////////f0///a0                   [serial]

010        $a    87600486 //r88
020        $a 0844405957 (loose-leaf)
245   00   $a USMARC format for bibliographic data : $b including guidelines
           for content designation / $c prepared by Network Development and
           MARC Standards Office.
260        $a Washington : $b Cataloging Distribution Service, Library of
           Congress, $c 1988-
300        $a 2 v. (loose-leaf) ; $c 28 cm.
```

Example 6
Serial Controlled Archivally

Archivists traditionally have not distinguished monographs from serials to the extent that library catalogers have. With Format Integration, this distinction is much easier to indicate for those who want to do so. According to the definition in the USMARC Format for Leader byte 07, a collection is "a made-up multipart group of items that were not originally published, distributed, or produced together." It would be incorrect, therefore, to code this record Leader byte 07 "c." Because the AMC 006 field currently contains only one defined byte of data (Form of Item), which also is defined in the Books and Serials 008/006 fields, it is likely that the AMC 006 field rarely will be used until additional bytes are defined. Also, the only currently valid value for 006/00 for AMC is "p" (Mixed Material). Since the model allows for AMC 006 fields for other than mixed material, this situation is under review.

Example 6A
Serial Controlled Archivally
Before Format Integration

```
LDR        *****nbc//22*****/a/4500                    [archival]
008        900823i19739999wiu/////////////////eng/d    [archival]

110   10   $a Wisconsin. $b Bureau of Local Financial Assistance.
245   00   $a Bulletin : $b municipal resources provided and expended, $f
           1973-[ongoing].
300        $a <2> $f c.f.
351        $b Alphabetical and chronological.
584        $a Accumulation: 0.1 c.f./year.
851        $3 current records $a Wisconsin Bureau of Local Financial
           Assistance
851        $3 semi-current records $a Wisconsin State Records Center
851        $3 non-current records $a Wisconsin State Archives
```

Example 6B
Serial Controlled Archivally
After Format Integration

```
LDR      *****nasa//22*****/a/4500              [serial]
008      900823c19739999wiuar////////s0/////eng/d   [serial]
006      p/////////////////                     [archival]


086      $a Rev.3/2:56- $2 widocs
110  1   $a Wisconsin. $b Bureau of Local Financial Assistance.
245  00  $a Bulletin : $b municipal resources provided and expended, $f
         1973-[ongoing].
300      $a <2> $f c.f.
310      $a Annual
351      $b Alphabetical and chronological.
584      $a Accumulation: 0.1 c.f./year. $5 WHi
852      $3 current records $a Wisconsin Bureau of Local Financial
         Assistance
852      $3 semi-current records $a Wisconsin State Records Center
852      $3 non-current records $a Wisconsin State Archives
```

Example 7
Serial Kit

This type of material is becoming more and more common and is handled much more easily with Format Integration, primarily because the choice of variable fields no longer is restricted. The July 1990 definitions of "kit" and "mixed material" in Leader byte 06 are problematic; the Library of Congress is attempting to resolve this problem.

Example 7A
Serial Kit
Before Format Integration
(cataloged in the Serials format)

```
LDR        *****nas//22*****/a/4500                      [serial]

008        910808c19919999mduqr1p//////0uuua0eng/b       [serial]

022   0    $a 1052-2174
032        $a 006565 $b USPS
042        $a nsdp $a lcd
210   0    $a Video j. echocardiogr.
222   00   $a Video journal of echocardiography
245   00   $a Video journal of echocardiography $h [kit].
260   00   $a Silver Spring, MD : $b Dynamedia, Inc., $c c1991-
265        $a Dynamedia Inc., 2 Fulham Ct., Silver Spring MD  20902
300        $a v.,     videocassettes.
310        $a Quarterly
350        $a $225.00
362   0    $a Vol. 1, no. 1 (Jan. 1991)-
500        $a VHS.
530        $a Videocassettes also issued in PAL and NTSC formats.
780   01   $t Dynamic cardiovascular imaging $x 0891-9313 $w (DLC)sn
           87000003
```

Example 7B
Serial Kit
Before Format Integration
(cataloged in the Visual Materials format)

```
LDR        *****nom//22*****/a/4500                    [visual materials]
[or (depending on system restrictions)]
LDR        *****nos//22*****/a/4500                    [visual materials]

007        vf/cbahou                                   [video cassette]
008        910808m19919999mdunnn///////////0bneng/b    [visual materials]

042        $a nsdp $a lcd
245  00    $a Video journal of echocardiography $h [kit].
260        $a Silver Spring, MD : $b Dynamedia, Inc., $c c1991-
265        $a Dynamedia Inc., 2 Fulham Ct., Silver Spring MD  20902
300        $a v. : $b ill. (some col.) ; $c 28 cm.
[300       $a videocassettes : $b sd., col. ; $c 1/2 in.
or
300        $a v.,    videocassettes.]
500        $a Quarterly; v. 1, no. 1 (Jan. 1991)-
580        $a Continues in part: Dynamic cardiovascular imaging.
500        $a VHS.
530        $3 Videocassettes $a also issued in PAL and NTSC formats.
500        $a ISSN 1052-2174 = Video journal of echocardiography.
```

Example 7C
Serial Kit
After Format Integration
(cataloged in the Visual Materials format)

```
LDR         *****nos22*****/a/4500
007         vf|cbahou                                        [video cassette]
008         910808c19919999mdunnn////////////bneng/b        [visual materials]
006         sqr1p///////0///a0                               [serial]

032         $a 006565 $a USPS
037         $b Dynamedia Inc., 2 Fulham Ct., Silver Spring MD  20902 $c
            225.00
042         $a nsdp $a lcd
022    0    $a 1052-2174
210    0    $a Video j. echocardiogr.
222    0    $a Video journal of echocardiography
245   00    $a Video journal of echocardiography $h [kit].
260         $a Silver Spring, MD : $b Dynamedia, Inc., $c c1991-
300         $a v. : $b ill. (some col.) ; $c 28 cm.
[300        $a videocassettes : $b sd., col. ; $c 1/2 in.
or
300         $a v.,    videocassettes.]
310         $a Quarterly
362    0    $a Vol. 1, no. 1 (Jan. 1991)-
538         $a VHS.
530         $3 Videocassettes $a also issued in PAL and NTSC formats.
780   01    $t Dynamic cardiovascular imaging $x 0891-9313 $w (DLC)sn
            87000003
```

Training Issues

Laura Kimberly

When Format Integration is implemented at the end of 1993, training for cataloging staff will bridge the gap between the concept of Format Integration and its application in the library. Ask a professional trainer for the definition of training and he or she likely will tell you that training is change in behavior. A regular contributor to *Training* magazine says, "Training changes uninformed employees into informed employees; training changes unskilled or semiskilled workers into employees who can do their tasks in 'the right way.' This 'right way' is called a standard."[1] To train workers in the right way, you first define the standard and then analyze what the worker already knows. Training aims at the difference between the standard and the worker's current knowledge and bridges this gap by providing the time and material needed for learning. Finally, you evaluate the training process itself.

Defining Training Needs

Since we already have the standard—the integrated USMARC format—we can turn to needs analysis. The training needs will be different for different institutions and for individual staff. Some staff members need to know how to interpret the USMARC record, others need to know how to edit the records that have been contributed to a shared database, and still others need to know how to create and contribute original records. Sometimes library or database standards, or even personal standards, require that those original records meet stringent quality guidelines, whereas other times they do not. Factors influencing those needs include how many other jobs the catalogers do, how many and what kinds of items the institution purchases, and the resources available to the catalogers. Not least in defining training needs is what the patrons expect of the bibliographic data the library offers them.

Table 1, "Format Issues," provides a framework for analyzing the specific skills the catalogers may need to learn for Format Integration.[2] This worksheet lists some basic competencies in Format Integration for cataloging staff, from minimum competencies to higher level competencies. To fill out this chart for your institution, first determine the importance of each competency for your library, then identify the specific learning need. For example, is this a completely new skill or an update of an existing skill? Is passing familiarity sufficient, or is a high level of expertise necessary? Table 1 is not necessarily a complete list, and you may want to rank skills differently at your institution.

You may begin your analysis with the question, "If all I catalog is books, do I even need to pay attention to Format Integration?" The answer is "yes." At minimum, there is a shift in the way alternative titles are tagged and the obsolescence of certain content designators. Also, catalogers need to recognize changed field names.

As you continue your analysis, you might list the 006 fields and determine the importance of learning each one based on the types of materials your library collects or that your staff are assigned to catalog. Although 006 fields (Fixed-Length Data Elements—Additional Material Characteristics) mirror the 008 fields (Fixed-Length Data Elements), you may need to train a highly specialized cataloger to code one or more types of material with which he or she is unfamiliar, such as an audiovisual cataloger who has not yet had the opportunity to attend to seriality.

In addition to the basic competencies, you must train people in decision-making skills. For example, a cataloger will need to distinguish between old and new records. And there will be many decisions relating to the use of 008 and 006 fields, as Anne Highsmith discusses in her paper.

You also should assess the need to relearn the cataloging rules that allow for the description of the multiple physical characteristics of an item. You may decide that no further training is needed in this area, but it still is best to include this question in your analysis of training needs.

Impact of Systems on Training

After analyzing the learning needs based on Format Integration, you can turn to system issues and their impact on training. Table 2, "System Issues," is designed to help you focus on how you think about database and screen design, system conversion, and documentation in the training context.

USMARC records are available from a variety of services, including the Cataloging Distribution Service of the Library of Congress, Baker and Taylor, Bibliofile, Marcive, OCLC, RLIN, and WLN. Your library may use one source or a combination of sources. Also, your staff may contribute records to more than one database. You can expand the model to include all the systems with which your staff interact in their cataloging activities.

In addition to the new intellectual activities related to the application of the USMARC format, Format Integration may bring about system changes that will alter the way you interact with the system. Training must take this into account. System changes also may impact the effort needed to learn the new format. If your staff can look at the screen and it prompts them for the information in terminology they can understand, it will take less time and energy and less formal training to learn.

Utilities and vendors will make other decisions about database and screen design in such areas as indexing, input screens or workforms, and validation. The ability to set cataloging and searching parameters based on new fields such as the 006 field could affect greatly the local system environment. Changes to indexing affect retrieval and reference use of the database. Thus, a list of competencies similar to those in Table 1 could be developed to analyze the training needs of yet another constituency of the USMARC format, the public services staff.

Conversion is a database design issue that receives a lot of emphasis, so I have placed it in a separate category. Issues related to conversion include the capability to include the 006 and other newly defined or redefined fields and the treatment of obsolete elements in the cataloging module. If your system does not convert older records or allow for post-Format Integration changes or additions to the older records, the ability to recognize obsolete codes becomes a more important competency.

Documentation and Training

The issue of documentation links the discussion of needs and training methods. Some people can learn solely from documentation, whereas others learn best in a classroom situation. At the least, documentation should provide information about specific applications of the standard. At its best, documentation will minimize the impact of this implementation. In looking at documentation issues, you will want to ask the following questions. What documentation does your system provide, and how does that impact training and the resources required for you to learn? Do you rely on *USMARC Format for Bibliographic Data*? Do you rely on separate format manuals for separate types of material or on one format manual? Apparently, separate manuals are a thing of the past. Both RLG and WLN currently provide consolidated format documentation, and OCLC is heading in that direction. What will be available to you at the time you implement Format Integration? How much effort will it take to learn to use the new documentation?

Training Methods

The methods for changing a worker's level from uninformed to informed, from unskilled to skilled, are many. The choice of method depends on how your staff learn, how much they need to learn, and the resources—money, time, and materials—available to you. At least three training methods should be available for Format Integration:

1. discovery and self-instruction that rely on documentation and system design,
2. instructor-led training sessions, and
3. self-instructional materials such as workbooks, audiovisual materials, and computer media.

Computer-based training software or videos, as well as satellite video teleconferencing, would be cost-effective media for providing Format Integration training to the large, far-reaching audience interested in this subject.

As trainers determine what methods to develop, they will be, consciously or unconsciously, examining traditions involving the current environment and resources. Table 3, "Trainer Issues," gives a sample of some of the factors that affect training from the trainer's viewpoint.

For the utilities, traditions have been influenced by a number of different factors, including:

- master record vs. cluster records and local practice considerations,
- the distribution of quality control processes (i.e., whether or not the user can change the master record),
- the structure of the documentation, and
- the needs of the utilities' users and their relationship to their users (for

example, recognizing that OCLC distributes services through regional networks that provide support and training).

Traditions vary among the library associations, library schools, local systems vendors, and local institutions. Some local systems vendors include tagging in their system training, whereas others assume that their users receive that training from their utility or another provider.

Format Integration also affects the curriculum of the library school, where the tradition is to teach theoretical principles rather than specific applications. The principles of Format Integration need to be integrated into library school cataloging courses. The approach to teaching in individual schools will depend on the resources available—does the school have access to OCLC, RLIN, or WLN? Thus, traditions, environment, and resources influence one another.

One of the traditions of teaching tagging is a tag-by-tag tour of the USMARC formats. For example, regional networks have provided separate tours of the manuals describing specific types of material format for OCLC users, whereas WLN generally has provided a tour of the consolidated format manual supplemented by optional courses on specific material types. Because material-specific issues will remain, we can anticipate that training on tagging for specialized types of materials will continue. In recent years, a few of the OCLC regional networks have begun teaching tagging based on a tour of the cataloging rules and relating them to USMARC tags. Whether Format Integration will encourage more use of this approach remains to be seen.

We also must look at the social context of our training. This major change to the USMARC formats is taking place in an environment of hard economic times, increasing local system installations, constantly changing technology, and concern over the future of the library school. In addition, every user must learn at about the same time. Some need transitional training, whereas others still need fundamental training in cataloging and tagging. The environment will change, of course, as Format Integration becomes the USMARC format and loses its newness.

Notes

1. David Laird, "Why Have a Training and Development Department Anyway," in *Designing and Delivering Cost Effective Training*, ed. Ron Zemke, Linda Standke, and Philip Jones (Minneapolis: Training Books, 1981), 17.
2. Loosely adapted from Minnesota Office of Library Development and Services, *Self-Assessment Guide for Cataloging* (Chicago: American Library Association, Continuing Library Education Network and Exchange Round Table, 1986).

Table 1. Training Format Issues

Name _____

Competencies	Importance	Learning Needs/Method
Tag an alternative title		
Recognize an obsolete tag		
Code 006—Books		
Code 006—Serials		
Code 006—Visual Materials		
Code 006—Archival and Manuscripts Control		
Code 006—Maps		
Code 006—Music		
Code 006—Computer Files		
...		
Distinguish old and new records		
Determine Type of Record		
Determine Bibliographic Level		
Determine when to apply 006 field		

Table 2. Training
System Issues

Source(s) of USMARC Records _____
Local System Vendor _____

	Source of Records	Local System	Time Tables	Impact on Training Needs
Database and Screen Design				
Retrieval				
Divided files				
Input screens				
Workforms				
Validation				
Conversion				
Capability to include 006 added retrospectively and/or prospectively				
Obsoletes removed				
Documentation				
Integrated or separate				
Revision or update pages				
Historical information				

Table 3. Training
Trainer Issues—Examples

	Traditions	*Environment*	*Resources*
General Factors		need for less costly training, for example: av, cbt; need for transitional training; system changes and conversions	staffing/volunteers; materials; financial
OCLC & Regional Networks	master record; quality control: central/distributed; separate	system changes; documentation changes; small–large users	network staff; OCLC staff; peer trainers
RLG	cluster records/local practice; distributed quality control; emphasis on system training	large users; specialized users	
WLN	master record; quality control: manual review; consolidated format: tag-by-tag tour	small users	
Local System Vendors	system training only and/or format training	variety of users with variety of needs	rely on utilities/networks for general format training
Local Institution	rely on utility/vendor programs or develop in-house training; highly specialized staff or generalized		financial; in-house experts; network, utility, or other training provider
Library Schools	theoretical principles; USMARC; systems available		
Library Associations	determined by members; sponsor programs		volunteers; financial

Documentation

Sally H. McCallum

An essential component of nationwide implementation of changes to a commonly used standard is documentation. For USMARC, all implementors must be working from exactly the same specifications or our ability to interchange data easily will be lost. The job of documenting USMARC falls on the Library of Congress as maintenance agency for USMARC.

The Library of Congress has produced two types of documents since the approval of the Format Integration proposal package in July 1988. The most important is the orderly incorporation of the changes in the USMARC format documentation. In addition, the Library of Congress has produced extra "road map" documents that assist in planning for implementation. The following describes the documentation and indicates how it may be obtained.

Road Maps

In December of 1988 *Format Integration and Its Effect on the USMARC Bibliographic Format* was published. This convenient 94-page document gave a summary of the decisions in the basic proposal, provided a history of the process (indicating its depth and breadth), clarified the model for the unified formats, indicated reasons for types of changes, contained a table to show all the changes, and included appendixes in which they were summarized.

This document facilitated understanding of the total change and planning for implementation.

From 1989 to 1991 several activities took place that mandated a new edition of this document as the community looked toward the final implementation date of 1994. A few items that could not be decided completely in the original format integration proposal finally were settled in 1989. A few other format changes from 1989 to 1991 that were viewed as disruptive were delayed until the implementation of Format Integration, while the deleted data elements and several of the data elements that had been made obsolete were implemented in 1988 and 1991, respectively.

In the summer of 1992 a new edition of *Format Integration and Its Effect on the USMARC Bibliographic Format* was published, updated to reflect the above changes. This is a valuable tool for implementors since it provides a convenient summary and clear description of the model that was used by the USMARC Advisory Committee in working out Format Integration.

USMARC Format

The USMARC formats issued by the Network Development and MARC Standards Office at the Library of Congress are the definitive specifications for the USMARC standards. Great care has been taken to produce an orderly progression of updates to the *USMARC Format for Bibliographic Data* as parts of Format Integration were implemented while other changes to the format continued to be made. The USMARC updates also serve a timing function. Approved format changes should not be made to systems until at least three months after the specifications for the changes are issued in a USMARC update. The following updates to *USMARC Format for Bibliographic Data* contain information pertaining to Format Integration.

Update No. 1 (November 1988)—Contained the deleted data elements that had been approved in July 1988.

Update No. 2 (August 1989)—A "Future" section was added to each field or data element that was to be changed. This section, at the end of the field description, reminded implementors and format developers alike of coming changes. The specifications in the "Future" section, however, are not yet valid to implement.

Update No. 3 (October 1990)—Several changes, the implementation of which was considered "nondisruptive" to systems, were moved out of the "Future" sections and into the field specifications. These changes involved primarily data elements that were reverting to undefined (coded in the future with a blank) and fields or subfields that would cease to be used, such as subfield ‡z (Source of Note Information) in the 5XX notes.

The final documentation of the integrated format will be published by the Library of Congress in the summer of 1993 in the form of a new edition of the bibliographic format. The elimination of all the "Future" sections and incorporation of the changes into the field specifications will cause many pages to change. The new edition eliminates interfiling a very large update and provides the opportunity to streamline the document, compressing it into two binders again. The designations beside each data element that show whether the element is valid for each form of material will be eliminated. (These designations also indicate whether the data element is required or optional for a national-level record.) This information will be contained in an appendix indicating "mandatory" and "mandatory if applicable" data elements for full national-level records, similar to the current appendix showing mandatory data elements for minimal national-level records.

The new edition will be the basis for future development of the format and will allow implementors finally to take advantage of Format Integration. As is the case with any update, issuance of the new edition allows that records containing the changes specified therein may start to appear in three months (and warns users that the changes are coming)—but, as usual, does not require an agency to make these changes.

Where to Obtain Documentation

The *USMARC Format for Bibliographic Data*, its Updates, and *Format Integration and Its Effect on the USMARC Bibliographic Format* can be obtained from the Cataloging Distribution Service, Library of Congress, Washington, DC 20541.

The Utilities

Jo Calk

This paper describes some implementation options and decisions facing the bibliographic utilities (OCLC, RLIN, and WLN). Although each of the major utilities is different, there are several areas that need to be addressed by each:

- Indexing
- Database conversion
- Impact on products

Indexing Considerations

Some of the changes introduced by Format Integration impact the indexing and display of bibliographic records. Rather than list all of the possible changes, the following specific examples will illustrate three different types of indexing problems:

1. Variable fields
2. Fixed-length fields
3. Leader and control data

Variable Fields

One of the most noticeable Variable field changes introduced by Format Integration is the use of the field 246 (Varying Form of Title) for titles for the item being cataloged other than those specifically provided for in fields 210 through 245. This type of other title information formerly was carried in field 740 (Added Entry—Variant Title). With Format Integration, field 740 has been renamed "Added Entry—Uncontrolled Related/Analytical Title," and is to be used only for titles for other related works and for titles contained within the item for which the record is being made.

Field 246, formerly reserved for serials, carries more indexing "intelligence" than field 740. The first indicator specifies whether a note should be printed and whether an added entry should be made—that is, whether the field should be indexed. The second indicator specifies the type of other title and is used to display the appropriate display constant. For example, in the field

```
246 11 $a Gramatica comercial bilingüe
```

first indicator "1" specifies that an Added Entry field is to be created, and second indicator "1" identifies this as a parallel title. In the field

```
246 10 $a Dictionary of troublesome words
```

first indicator "1" specifies that an Added Entry field is to be created, and second indicator "0" identifies this as a portion of a title.

Because field 246 has been used in serial bibliographic records for years, implementing this type of indexing change should not be a major problem for the utilities. However, other changes introduced by Format Integration could bring about some major headaches.

Fixed-Length Fields

The utilities have been indexing (or at least qualifying searches) by one or more of the elements in the 008 field (Fixed-Length Data Elements) for a long time. For example, online systems or CD-ROM catalogs use data from the 008 field to limit searches by language, government publication, target audience, and date.

The 008 field is format-specific: there is a Books 008 field, a Serials 008 field, a Maps 008 field, etc. Format Integration will not change that. Currently, when cataloging a map serial, the cataloger must choose either to consider the item a map and use the Map 008 field or to consider it a serial and use the Serials 008 field. If the Serials 008 field were selected, then coded information such as "relief" and "projection" would be lost. If the Map 008 field were selected, coded information such as "frequency" and "regularity" would be lost.

However, Format Integration will allow the cataloger to record coded information about the map aspects of a map serial as well as the serial aspects of a map serial. This was done by adding the 006 field (Fixed-Length Data Elements—Additional Material Characteristics). Now the cataloger only needs to determine whether to use the Map 008 and the Serial 006 fields or the Serial 008 and the Map 006 fields.

Although it is expected that there will be few 006 fields, the utilities need to determine what access will be provided to the 006 field. Will it be indexed like the 008 field? Will it be considered an "extension" of the 008 field? Or will it be a separate field indexed in conjunction with, or subsequent to, the indexing of the 008 field?

The 006 field is a new field. Although the 007 (Physical Description Fixed Field) has been defined and used for several years, most of the processing, including indexing, treats the 007 field as a separate field from the 008. Now the utilities will have two "008-like" fields in the record, vying for attention. It is expected that the utilities will adjust their indexing and display programs to accommodate fixed-field information derived from both the 008 and 006 fields.

Leader and Control Fields

The utilities also have been indexing (or at least qualifying searches) by one or more of the elements in the Leader for a long time. For example, online systems or CD-ROM catalogs that limit searches by type of material (books, serials, maps, etc.) use data from the Leader. If a user wants to limit his or her search to maps, currently the most common way to do so is by using the code in Leader byte 6 (Type of Record). However, as illustrated in Example 2 in "Multimedia Materials," this method would miss a map that is a puzzle. Therefore, with Format Integration, searches could be limited by a combination of Leader byte 6 and the first character of the 006 field.

Some systems also divide their files by the type of material, using the Type of Record and Bibliographic Level elements from the Leader. Before Format Integration, an archival or a manuscripts control record was identified by Leader byte 6 Type of Record code "b." With Format Integration, the archival perspective can apply to any format. For example, one can catalog a map serial that is archivally controlled. This change involves defining the previously undefined Leader byte 8 to Type of Control and setting code "a."

Utilities that had been using Leader byte 6 Type of Record (and, occasionally, Leader byte 7 Bibliographic Level—for example, for serials) now have to include Leader byte 8 Type of Control when searching for an archival or a manuscripts control item. Although this change sounds relatively easy, the introduction of Leader byte 8 to the USMARC format is perhaps one of the biggest retooling "opportunities" for utilities and other systems. (I often am told that challenges are "opportunities in disguise," so I am using that term.)

Many programs that handle a bibliographic record that is received on tape use the Leader bytes to determine how to process the information. That is why the information is stored at the beginning of the MARC format bibliographic record. Utilities and systems will have to determine whether they want to retool these basic systems to identify archival and manuscript control materials, or to continue looking at Leader bytes 6 and 7 only, with the end result that the "archivalness" of the item is lost.

Database Conversion

Utilities are faced with a problem: They cannot convert the database before the end of 1993 because none of the local systems will be ready for the new data elements. However, if they are expected to start distributing records with the new data elements on January 1, 1994, it is highly unlikely that any of the utilities will be able to convert their entire database overnight, between December 31, 1993, and January 1, 1994.

In addition, utilities must be concerned about the various local systems used by their members. Will the local systems be able to change in time? Will records have to be reissued by the utility and reloaded on the local system? Or will the records be converted (or at least "handled") on the local system?

Therefore, each utility faces several decisions affecting the database:

• What does "database conversion" mean, anyway?
• What if we do not convert the database?
• If we do convert the database, how will we do it?

What Does "Database Conversion" Mean, Anyway?

As mentioned earlier, there are four kinds of changes involved in Format Integration:

1. Deleted content designators. These were not used in the past and should not be used now. An example is field 330 (Publication Pattern) in serials. Because this kind of change probably involves only changes to validation tables, no database conversion is needed.

2. Obsolete content designators. These are not to be used in current input (i.e., current or retrospective conversion), but may continue to appear

in older records. Examples include the second indicator (Main Entry/ Subject Relationship) of fields 1XX (Main Entry) and field 570 (Editor Note) in serials. If a utility converts these data elements in its database, the utility also will have to convert every record before loading it into the "clean" database. Because LC will not convert its database, and because obsolete data elements are allowed in older records, utilities may decide not to convert obsolete content designators.

3. New content designators. Since most of the "new" data elements are actually changes to existing data elements, this involves more than simply adding the data elements to validation tables. These are likely candidates for conversion. Some examples of "new" content designators include:
   - byte 32, which is "Undefined" for Books, Music, and Visual Materials. It appears on the obsolete content designators list as 008 byte 32 (Main Entry in Body of Entry)
   - field 260 (Publication, Distribution, Etc.). The "new" first and second indicators are defined as blank, but the original values for field 260 first and second indicators appear on the obsolete content designator list.

4. Name changes. Although most of the name changes primarily affect documentation, some are actually format changes in disguise (e.g., changing the definition of "blank" in Leader byte 8 from "Undefined" to "No specified type of control," and changing the name of field 740 from "Added Entry—Variant Title" to "Added Entry—Uncontrolled Related/Analytical Title"). Some of these changes are likely candidates for conversion.

There are other changes that also can be made during a database conversion:

- Addition of data elements, such as fields 003 (Control Number Identifier), 005 (Date and Time of Latest Transaction), and 040 (Cataloging Source), which now are required.
- Cleanup of older obsolete or deleted data elements that had not yet been changed in the utility's database, such as the "desuperimposition" of 008 field changes.
- Cleanup of nonstandard practices and idiosyncracies. Any time someone mentions "database conversion," people come up with hundreds of ideas for additional changes to be included in the package. The danger is that sometimes the package gets so heavy from these additional changes that it is decided to scrap the idea of converting the database at all.

What If Utilities Do Not Convert the Database?

If utilities do not convert the database, they could force a gradual upgrading of older records by removing the obsolete data elements from the validation tables. When someone edits the record, the obsolete data element would be flagged as an error and the person would have to correct the data element before concluding the record editing. Alternatively, the obsolete data elements could be retained in the validation table, thus not requiring older records to be upgraded during editing.

If the database is not converted, will the utility try to convert each individual record at the time that it is distributed or downloaded? Or will the records be distributed or downloaded without being converted to Format Integration? Unconverted records can cause problems in receiving systems. For example, if the utility does not convert the Leader in an archival record from Leader byte 6 (Type of Record) code "b" to Leader byte 8 (Type of Control) code "a," local systems receiving the record may not recognize it as an archival record.

If Utilities Do Convert the Database, How Will They Do It?

Can the utilities "tweak" each record online? Or do they have to unload the database, convert it, and reload it? Or do they make it look like it has been converted by changing the display of the record? For example, do they display and output the 260 indicators as blanks, regardless of the value in the online record? Do they take the utility down for a week or so while they are converting the database? Or do they keep the system up in a "read-only" mode while converting the database offline?

There is no "right" answer to these questions, but these are some of the choices the utilities must make. Each utility has to decide the approach that is best suited to its customers and products.

Impact on Products

The term *products* is used rather loosely to include cards, COM, CD-ROM, printed shelflists and other printed reports, downloaded records from the database or CD-ROM, validation tables and online validation, linked files (such as Authority, Acquisitions, Holdings, ILL), input screens, interface with workstations, Internet access, etc.

There are two basic paths, depending on whether the utility converts the database or not.

If the Utility Converts the Database

Utilities must look into the various internal programs, tables, and modules that produce the products, and make the appropriate changes to allow the use of new data elements. If obsolete data elements also have been converted, the products modules can be changed to no longer allow obsolete data elements.

If the Utility Does Not Convert the Database

Utilities must look into the various internal programs, tables, and modules that produce the products, and make the appropriate changes to allow the use of new data elements as well as old data elements.

Utilities must determine whether records will need to be converted "on the fly" before they are distributed on the product. For example, are people expecting to download "format-integrated" bibliographic records from the online system or CD-ROM catalog? Or will the records be distributed "as is," with only newly input records conforming to Format Integration specifications?

Conclusion

The utilities do not make these decisions in a vacuum. Each utility has to determine the resources available for what could be a substantial amount of work with little or no monetary gains. Because they probably will not charge more for "format-integrated" records, the utilities themselves will have to absorb the costs of implementation. Also, the Library of Congress is the largest single contributor to the utilities' databases. If LC does not convert its files, the utility probably would be less inclined to convert its database because each record added after the conversion must be "format-integrated" before being loaded.

All of the utilities are committed to implementing Format Integration, but each must determine how much it can afford to do. As each utility faces these and other options in implementing Format Integration, it will solicit input from its users and notify the users of plans and decisions as they are made.

Although Format Integration is one of the largest conversion projects recently undertaken by the library automation community, it provides an opportunity to simplify the USMARC formats and, in turn, help simplify cataloging and retrieval of library data.

Local Systems

Priscilla Caplan

The similarity of issues to be faced by the bibliographic utilities and by those responsible for local library systems is one measure of how much the world has changed. It was not that long ago when only the Library of Congress and the utilities needed to worry about creating USMARC records and exporting them to other systems. Conversely, only local systems were concerned with importing foreign records and displaying bibliographic data to the public.

Today, nearly all of the cataloging functions of the utilities also are performed locally, whereas the utilities are experimenting with reference services targeted at the end-user. Exchange of data takes place in both directions, with many institutions tapeloading their local cataloging to one or more of the utilities even as they download data from the utilities.

What this means in the context of Format Integration is that almost all the concerns relevant to the utilities also must be addressed by vendors and developers of local systems. At the same time, librarians who manage and run local systems should understand what these issues are and take the initiative in finding out from their vendors what their plans are.

There are several good reasons that local system managers should discuss Format Integration with their vendors as early as possible, not the least of which is to reassure themselves that their vendors do indeed have plans for coping with Format Integration, a likely but still comforting event. In addition, knowing what the vendors aim to do will give users time to prepare for the changes, or at least to plan for when they will have to allocate staff time for such tasks as installation, training, and redocumentation. Also, at least at the time of this writing, most vendors' plans are still fluid and could be influenced by users with strong preferences.

What follows is a list of areas affected by Format Integration, with notes on issues raised and options for dealing with them. Those responsible for managing local systems might want to use this as a starting point for discussion, both with their vendor and with the library staff who depend on the local system to do their work.

Data Validation

Many local systems use validation tables to verify the correctness of content designation (field tags, subfield codes, values for fixed fields and indicators). Such systems are likely to use a separate table for each format. Extensive changes to validation tables will be required to accommodate Format Integration, especially the extension of usable fields across all formats. At the very least, the tables for each format will have to be updated to include the new tags and values. In some systems, tables could be redesigned to consolidate the rules for variable fields into a single list. In either case, any documentation pertaining to local system validation must be reproduced or reissued.

A second consideration is the handling of obsolete content designation. Obsolete fields and values in USMARC can remain in older records but cannot be entered into new ones. Most validation tables, however, do not make this distinction. A local system may not allow an operator to edit a field containing obsolete content designation without correcting the field, or it might not allow editing of any field in that record without correcting the invalid one. The system should, however, allow the display of obsolete data and editing of the record containing such data.

A number of little-used content designators have already been made obsolete in Update No. 3 (October 1990) to the _USMARC Format for Bibliographic Data._ These include the 008 byte 32 (Main Entry in Body of Entry) in Books, Music, and Visual Materials; the first indicator of the 222 field (Key Title) in Serials and Computer Files, and the 320 field (Page Count) in Books. Checking how a local system implemented these changes probably will provide a good clue as to how it handles obsolete content designation in general.

The 006 Field

The 006 field (Fixed-Length Data Elements—Additional Material Characteristics), like the 007 field (Physical Description Fixed Field), is an odd hybrid. It is like the fixed fields, such as the Leader and 008 field (Fixed-Length Data Elements), in that it consists of coded data, positionally defined, but it is like the variable fields in that it may or may not occur one or more times in a record. This makes data entry for the 006 field an interesting problem for local systems.

One alternative is to offer a workform (or rather, seven workforms, one for each type of 006 field) where each data element is labeled separately for data entry. If this is the approach, there must be some way of requesting the appropriate workform, since unlike the 008 field values, catalogers would not want to see a screen of these every time they created a bibliographic record. A second approach requires entering the values as a single string as though it were a variable field. In this case, individual data elements within the 006 field may or may not be separated with subfield codes. Regardless of how it is entered, each data element within the 006 field should be validated separately.

The way a system treats the 007 field could be a clue as to how the system vendor is planning to handle the 006 field. Figure 1 shows contrasting ways of treating 007 fields in two of the bibliographic utilities, OCLC and RLIN.

Importing and Exporting USMARC Records

Most local systems can import bibliographic records from the utilities or other sources either as batch loads or in real-time data transfer, or both. It goes without saying that if any special programs are used to reformat data for loading or transfer, these programs should be able to handle records containing post-Format Integration content designation. Since not all the utilities are planning currently to convert their existing databases, these programs also must be able to handle records containing pre-Format Integration data. The latter actually may be more difficult than the former for local systems that strip any incoming fields not found in the current data validation tables.

If a system performs automatic duplicate detection between incoming records and those already in the database, additional issues arise. Will the system consider records in different USMARC formats to be duplicates? Would local staff want it to? With Format Integration, it would be possible for two catalogers to catalog the same item in different formats, but this would be unlikely in most cases, given the rules for selecting the primary format.

In systems allowing real-time import of USMARC records, it may be possible to designate an existing record as a target. The target simply may be overlayed by the incoming data, or a more sophisticated process of combination may take place. Will the local system combine duplicates in different formats? If records in different formats were to be combined, decisions would have to be made about which would become the primary format and whether to create an 006 field for the other.

Many local systems can export USMARC records for reporting to the bibliographic utilities, contributing to union lists, etc. If at all possible, a system should be able to export all data, whether created before or after Format Integration.

Index Search and Display

Some local systems include format information index entries or very brief records displayed in response to a search. In NOTIS, for example, a combination of the Form of Reproduction Code (REPRO) and the Record Type (RT) is used to generate a display constant called the "medium descriptor." In HOLLIS, a display constant is generated based on Record Type and Bibliographic Level Codes. Figure 2 shows Format Information displayed in NOTIS and HOLLIS indexes. Any system that uses Record Type in this way must now take into account the two new Record Types, "p" and "t," as well as the obsolescence of type "b." Also, system designers should consider whether to display more than one format literal when a record reflects more than one format (i.e., it contains one or more 006 fields). As a variation on this, one slot might be reserved for seriality and one for other format information.

Many systems also allow string or keyword searches to be limited by format, in the sense that a searcher can indicate that only serials, maps, etc., should be included in the retrieval set. This probably is based on the primary format (the one represented by the 008 field), but it would be most useful if all formats were represented so that, for example, a serial map would be included both in searches limited to serials and in searches limited to maps. Depending on the system, this may require software development on the vendor's part to restructure the indexes. It also may require the local installation to run an index regeneration to reflect the change.

Screen Displays

Many online public access catalogs make no explicit mention at all of the format of displayed bibliographic records. Format information must be inferred from the description in field 300 (Physical Description), the General Material Designator, and other clues scattered thoughout the record. Figure 3 shows displays from some systems that do indicate format in their full or long display.

One could argue that Format Integration is hardly worth the bother if it has no effect on end-user access to and interpretation of bibliographic records. Format Integration gives the opportunity for major enhancements to the way multiformat materials are treated in the indexes to the public catalog, as noted above. OPAC screen displays also may be affected. Display specifications should be reviewed in systems that use display tables based on format. Designers of all systems should think about the public representation of the Record Type code and possibly other data from the 006 field. For the library running the local system, the biggest issue may be revising locally produced documentation, particularly if pictures of OPAC screens play a large role in handouts, materials for bibliographic instruction, or other public documentation.

Systems that provide a MARC-like display for staff also will have changes to screens. At the very least, the new data element for Type of Control will have to be placed with the fixed fields.

Format-Specific Functionality

Does the local system support any special processing or functionality based on format? Seriality is a likely culprit here. Is there any relationship between seriality and standing orders, check-in functions, or serial holdings statements? Are there special products for serials, such as periodicals lists for public areas? These features presumably should apply to those records for which seriality is a secondary characteristic, as well as to those for which it is primary (i.e., for records with serial 006 fields as well as those with serial 008 fields).

Some systems also may have special functions for materials treated archivally. After Format Integration, archival control no longer will be indicated by Record Type "b" in Leader byte 06, which is being made obsolete, but rather by a new data element defined for Type of Control in Leader byte 08. Any functions currently driven by Record Type will have to look both places for archival control unless the database is converted.

Reporting

Some systems allow "live file" reporting in which queries can be run directly against the bibliographic database. Other systems create reporting files containing information extracted from bibliographic records. In either case, it should be possible to do statistical reporting based on the new Type of Control code in the Leader and on the new 006 field.

Library managers also should examine whatever "canned" or preprogrammed reports are produced by the local system on a regular or an *ad hoc* basis. For example, there may be reports of acquisitions or expenditures by format. In all reports that involve format information, system managers should consider whether format information from the 006 field should be included. If it is, total counts will be inflated since some bibliographic records will be counted as more than one format. On the other hand, if 006 field information is not included, counts for each format will continue to be underrepresented; for example, the serial map will be counted in only one category.

File Conversion

As noted above, the requirement to permit obsolete content designation in older records while prohibiting it in newer ones can lead to some complexity in data validation, import, and export. It is tempting to try to eliminate some of the problems by converting the existing database to post-Format Integration content designation. There are several different cases to consider.

Newly defined or extended data elements are not relevant to such a conversion in most cases. The omission of a possibly relevant data element is not an error in content designation, and conversion programs are unlikely to be able to supply the relevant data, anyway. For example, field 256 (Computer File Characteristics) will be valid when applicable in all formats after Format Integration. However, if a cataloger cataloging an electronic journal as a serial failed to provide a field 256, it is extremely unlikely that any local system would either treat this as an error or try to supply a field 256 automatically.

Obsolete data elements can be converted in most cases. In general, obsolete indicator values can be set to an appropriate default. The data in obsolete fields and subfields ordinarily should not be stripped but rather moved to currently appropriate places. In some cases, this is straightforward—for example, retagging field 537 (Source of Data Note) as a field 500 (General Note). In other cases, it is more complicated, as when the data in field 265 (Source for Acquisition/Subscription Address) must be moved to the subfield ‡b of the newly redefined field 037 (Source of Acquisition).

Some special cases that will require extra attention include the obsolescence of Leader byte 06 (Type of Record) code "b," changes to Type of Date/Publication Status, Date 1 and Date 2 in the 008 bytes 06-14, and the redefinitions of fields 246 (Varying Form of Title) and 740 (Added Entry—Uncontrolled Related/Analytical Title).

Vendors may or may not recommend or provide programs for a complete or selective one-time retrospective conversion of bibliographic databases.

Conversion can simplify ongoing data validation and export routines. Conversion is useless, however, if the system continues to import records containing the older, pre-Format Integration content designation. Therefore, unless all sources of bibliographic data used by a system also plan to undergo a similar database conversion, programs that prepare data for importation to the system also must perform the same conversion functions on an ongoing basis.

Timing

Vendors may want to provide a phased implementation of new software related to Format Integration. Certainly, updated data validation tables, the ability to create and display 006 fields, and the ability to import and export bibliographic records with post-Format Integration content designation must be available for "Day 1." On the other hand, enhancements to the indexes, the reporting function, or public catalog displays probably could be delayed without harm.

Changes may come together in a "Format Integration package" or may be included with unrelated updates in a larger release. In either case, local system managers should make sure they have enough lead time to install and test the software, distribute documentation, and do all the other tasks a new release generally entails before the actual date of conversion that will be followed by LC and the utilities.

It also is important to determine whether installing the Format Integration changes will require an institution to run the current release of its local system software. This may be the case if the vendor decides to distribute the updates as a complete new release, as opposed to a series of patches to existing code. If so, and if an institution is not running the current release (whether by choice or for some other reason), managers also will have to consider the work required to achieve currency.

Conclusion

The important thing is to realize that it is not too early to plan for Format Integration. It is true that a few local system functions will be affected by implementation decisions made by LC and the utilities. If a local system imports records from a utility that decides not to do a retrospective conversion of its database, the system either will have to allow obsolete content designation or to provide programs to convert data on import. Most decisions, however, depend only on understanding the changes that Format Integration entails. This information is readily available in *Format Integration and Its*

Effect on the USMARC Bibliographic Format, prepared by the Library of Congress Network Development and MARC Standards Office. Armed with that guide, and perhaps with this manual, vendors and library managers of local systems should be able to enter into a productive dialogue in preparation for Format Integration.

OCLC

```
OCLC:  25004199           Rec stat:    n
  Entered:   19880629     Replaced:   19911220     Used:     19911220
> Type: a        Bib lvl: m      Source:  d       Lang: ita
  Repr: a        Enc lvl: M      Conf pub: 0      Ctry: it
  Indx: 0        Mod rec:        Govt pub:        Cont:
  Desc: a        Int lvl:        Festschr: 0      Illus:
                 F/B:     0      Dat tp:  r       Dates: 1865,1991 <
>  1  040     HMM $c HMM <
>  2  007     h $b d $c u $d b $e f $f a012 $g b $h a $i a $j a <
>  3  090     $b  <
>  4  049     HMMA <
>  5  100 0   Anonimo catanese. <
>  6  245 10  Vita di Giuseppe Garibaldi, dettata in ristretto / $c da un
anonimo catanese, 1807-1860. <
>  7  260     Catania : $b Stab. tip. Caronda, $c 1865. <
>  8  300     41 p. ; $c 24 cm. <
>  9  533     Microfilm. $b Cambridge, Mass. : $c Harvard University Library
Microreproduction Service, $d 1991. $e 1 microfilm reel : negative ; 35 mm. <
> 10  600 10  Garibaldi, Giuseppe, $d 1807-1882. <
```

RLIN

```
 ID:PAUG92-B53076          RTYP:c    ST:p   FRN:   MS:   EL:      AD:09-25-92
 CC:9112  BLT:am     DCF:a   CSC:d   MOD:   SNR:         ATC:     UD:09-25-92
 CP:enk   L:eng      INT:    GPC:    BIO:   FIC:1  CON:
 PC:s     PD:1992/           REP:    CPI:0  FSI:0  ILC:a   II:0
 MMD:     OR:   POL:   DM:    RR:           COL:         EML:   GEN:   BSE:
 010    GB9165555
 020    0521395763 :$cL4.25 (pbk.)
 040    Uk$cUk$dDLC$dCStRLIN
 100 1  Shakespeare, William,$d1564-1616.
 245 10 Othello /$cedited by Jane Coles.
 260    Cambridge :$bCambridge University Press,$c1992.
 300    236 p. :$bill. ;$c23 cm.
 490 1  Cambridge school Shakespeare
 520    An edition of Shakespeare's tragedy, including discussion of its
production, themes, patterns, language, and author.
 600 10 Shakespeare, William,$d1564-1616.$tOthello.
 700 10 Coles, Jane.
 800 1  Shakespeare, William,$d1564-1616.$tWorks.$f1991.$sCambridge
University Press.
```

Figure 1. 007 fields in OCLC and RLIN. Screen prints taken October 5, 1992.

Harvard's HOLLIS System

```
FIND TI OTHELLO
--------------------------------------------------------------------------O
THELLO
 1 davison peter hobley/ 1988  bks
 2 dvorak antonin 1841 1904/ 1894   sco
 3 dvorak antonin 1841 1904/ 1970   sco
 4 forrest edwin 1806 1872/ 1971  bks
 5 hauff wilhelm 1802 1827/ 1981  bks
 6 salgado fenella/ 1985  bks
 7 shakespeare william 1564 1616/ 1705  bks
 8 shakespeare william 1564 1616/ 1850  bks
 9 shakespeare william 1564 1616/ 1879  bks
10 shakespeare william 1564 1616/ 1885  bks
11 shakespeare william 1564 1616/ 1886  bks
12 shakespeare william 1564 1616/ 1908  bks
13 shakespeare william 1564 1616/ 1930  bks
14 shakespeare william 1564 1616/ 1941  bks
15 shakespeare william 1564 1616/ 1947  bks
```

Vanderbilt's NOTIS system ACORN

```
Search Request:  T=OTHELLO              ACORN
_____
      OTHELLO
 1  <—-> visual  (VU)
 2  <1984> visual  (VU)
 3   DAVISON PETER HOBLEY <1988>  (VU)
 4   SHAKESPEARE WILLIAM <—-> sound  (VU)
 5   SHAKESPEARE WILLIAM <1909>  (VU)
 6   SHAKESPEARE WILLIAM <1955>  (VU)
 7   SHAKESPEARE WILLIAM <1957>  (VU)
 8   SHAKESPEARE WILLIAM <1960> sound  (VU)
 9   SHAKESPEARE WILLIAM <1961>  (VU)
10   SHAKESPEARE WILLIAM <1962>  (VU)
11   SHAKESPEARE WILLIAM <1963> sound  (VU)
12   SHAKESPEARE WILLIAM <1968> microcard  (VU)
13   SHAKESPEARE WILLIAM <1968> microfilm  (VU)
14   SHAKESPEARE WILLIAM <1968> microfilm  (VU)
```

Figure 2. Showing format information in an index display. Screen prints taken
        October 5, 1992.

San Francisco State University's GEAC System

DETAILED DISPLAY

AUTHOR   :Verdi, Giuseppe, 1813-1901
                   Boito, Arrigo, 1842-1918
                   Otello
TITLE   :Othello (Otello) Oper in vier Akten von Arrigo Boito. Neue
                   deutsche Ubertragung von Walter Felsenstein, unter Mitarbeit
                   von Carl Stueber. Klavierauszug mit deutschem und
                   italienischem Text, nach dem Autograph der Partitur revidiert
                   von Mario Parenti (1964)
SUBJECT   :Operas — Vocal scores with piano
LANGUAGE   :GERMAN
MEDIA   :Music and Sound recordings
PUBLISHER   :[Mailand] Ricordi
PUB. DATE   :[1964, c1963]
DESCRIPTION   :xi, 300 p. illus., facsim. 27 cm.
NOTES   :Libretto by Boito.

Denver Public Library's CARL System

```
------------------------------------------------Denver Public Library-----
TITLE(s):         Othello [videorecording] /  BBC/Time-Life Films.

                  New York :  Ambrose Video Pub. [distributor],  c1988.
                  2 videocassettes (VHS) (203 min.) :  sd., col. ;  1/2 in.
                  The Shakespeare plays
                  Complete dramatic works of William Shakespeare
                  Dates vary: on cassette, c1982; publicity material, c1988.

                  Videocassette release of the 1982 production.
                  Anthony Hopkins, Bob Hoskins, Penelope Wilton.
Summary:          A dramatization of William Shakespeare's play Othello.
Format:           Video
Format:           Videocassettes.

OTHER ENTRIES:    Shakespeare, William,  1564-1616.   Othello.
                  Hopkins, Anthony,   1941-
                  Hoskins, Bob.
                  Wilton, Penelope,
                  British Broadcasting Corporation.
```

Figure 3. Showing format information in the public catalog. Screen prints taken
        October 5, 1992.

Online Public Access Catalogs

Karen Coyle

It is easy to understand why there is a lot of concern about Format Integration. Large, complex databases have been built on the unintegrated USMARC format, and a large number of library users have been trained, or have trained themselves, to use those databases. A change of the magnitude of Format Integration easily could throw the modern library world into chaos for years.

To our good fortune, Format Integration was designed by people who are well aware of this danger. Format Integration, although a major change in the concept of the USMARC record, actually leaves more alone than it changes. The vast majority of bibliographic records that are created will look the same after Format Integration as they would have before. The changes that do occur will take place primarily in particular categories of records that we can identify, such as nonprint serials and multimedia works. In addition, Format Integration was designed carefully to be, as the computer world terms it, "backwardly compatible." That means that built into the design of Format Integration is the recognition that pre-Format Integration records and post-Format Integration records must exist in the same bibliographic and system universe.

However, Format Integration cannot be ignored altogether. Whether a system will receive one record that makes use of Format Integration or one million, the system must be able to handle them. It is hoped that handling them is a small matter for the online public access catalog.

The Effect of Format Integration on the OPAC

The designers of Format Integration were prompted by difficulties that catalogers had experienced in coding certain materials into the USMARC formats. Cataloging is such an exacting art that it is easy to lose sight of the ultimate goal of the catalog record, which, to quote S.R. Ranganathan, is "Every user his book." The catalog record is the communication device that brings a user together with a library item. Difficulties in coding some kinds of materials also must translate into difficulties in helping users link to those materials. By unifying the coding of bibliographic formats in the USMARC record, the library world has taken a step toward unifying the bibliographic universe that its systems present to the user.

Most OPAC systems today place all materials in a single file for retrieval, with the possible exception of serials, which still sometimes are segregated from other materials. The assumption is that most users are looking for information about a topic—information that may be found in a variety of media. These unified files were implemented in OPACs even though the records themselves were created in separate USMARC formats. It was possible to combine these records because the majority of fields used for description and access were the same across formats. At the same time, systems had to make exceptions whenever data important for user access or display differed from one format to another; without exceptions, systems would lose some degree of user service. The point is that the user should not be limited in a search by the physical format of the items held by the library, but always should be aware of the format of items retrieved.

Format Integration states that each USMARC field has a precise meaning regardless of the format of the record itself. This means that a system can treat a field for searching or for display without examining the format of the record. The user should experience a consistency of treatment in all types of materials, and this supports the view that there is one universe of knowledge, with a variety of packaging options.

Effect on Searching

With the exception of the 006 field (Fixed-Length Data Elements—Additional Material Characteristics), Format Integration does not introduce new fields to the USMARC format. For that reason, its effect on searching should be negligible. Fields that now are indexed in OPACs tend to be fields that always have been valid across all formats: author fields, titles, subjects. Specialty fields, such as music publisher numbers or specialized notes, that were indexed by a system in the past, will continue to be indexed under Format Integration. The difference is that such indexing no longer should be limited to records with certain format codes in their Leaders. This means, for example, that the music publisher number or the map scale will be indexed in every record in which it is found in the database, not just those with bibliographic type "c" or "e."

The 006 field might change indexing for some records, depending on whether the system allows users to specify material formats in searches (e.g., FIND TITLE MONDO AND FORM VIDEO). Before Format Integration, each record expressed only a single format, although the repeatable 007 field (Physical Description Fixed Field) gave some additional format information. With Format Integration, the relevant fixed-field information formerly carried in the nonrepeatable 008 field (Fixed-Length Data Elements) is carried in the 006 field. This gives systems high-level information on more than one format, making more than one format available for searching.

Although this sounds like a change with far-reaching implications, it is important to remember that by far the greatest use of the 006 field will be to express seriality in records where the Leader code Bibliographic Level and the 008 field are for a nonprint item. Clearly, system designers must decide if these cases of seriality are to become part of the user view of the catalog. It is my opinion that few users are interested in the seriality aspect of a video, a score, or a map when they are searching online. Secondary material characteristics are more likely to be part of the user view when they represent additional formats in multimedia works. Access to seriality may well become one of those features installed in OPACs with the hope that the user will never find it; however, it will be available to the librarian who can understand its relation to the work.

Effect on Display

Basic Displays

The degree to which Format Integration will affect an OPAC's display depends on how format-specific the system's display is now. As with searching, the fields that are most commonly used for display are alike in all formats: author, title, publisher. In addition, most systems display much less than actually is carried in the full USMARC record in their primary user displays. Although long displays usually are available in the MELVYL® system at the University of California, more than 70 percent of all displays use the default display, a brief paragraph display much like the main paragraph of a catalog card (see Figure 1). Thus, the parts of the record that vary from one format to another are not the ones the user sees.

```
8. Hansten, Philip D.
      Drug interactions & updates / Philip D.
   Hansten, John R. Horn.  Malvern, Pa. : Lea &
   Febiger ; Vancouver, Wash. : Applied
   Therapeutics,  1990-
```

Figure 1. Default display

The longest user display in most systems includes all public information about the bibliographic item. These displays, if they currently vary based on record format, will have to change. If, on the other hand, fields are displayed from the record on their own merit, the user may be given additional data in a record, but the display system will be oblivious to the effect of Format Integration, since the fields themselves will not be new. In any case, the displays will not be any different from those the user has learned to read before Format Integration.

Displaying the Format

There is only one area where Format Integration might affect displays: in the display of the record format itself. In many systems, the displays identify the format of the item, especially for nonbooks (see Figure 2).

With additional information in the 006 field, more than one material type could be displayed in this area, but will systems choose to display multiple formats? Again, we need to remember that many of the 006 fields will indicate seriality of a nonbook format. That same seriality information is available in the records today as the bibliographic level "s" in the Leader. I have not seen a system that includes this seriality in its user displays, except where the bibliographic type is "print," and then the item simply is identified as "serial." For multimedia records, it may be useful to include more than one material type in the user display, but systems will have trouble finding space for more than a few medium designators in a display. If it is deemed important to alert users to all material types in the display, it might be necessary to include the relevant 3XX field in the basic user display. This, by the way, is as true today as it will be under Format Integration.

```
Biological abstracts on compact disc. 1990. COMPUTER FILE
```

Figure 2. Display with format

Format-Specific Displays

In the University of California's MELVYL system, we have made some concessions to format-specific displays, mainly for music libraries. Because of the emphasis on uniform titles in music cataloging, we substitute the uniform title for the title proper in our briefest display. We also sort on the uniform title instead of on the title proper for the music records. This kind of special processing need not be eliminated after Format Integration takes effect. The Leader value for bibliographic level still will tell us that the record is for a music item, either score or sound recording, and we can continue our special practice for this constituency.

At the same time, some common sense decisions for other display options must be made. For example, when our system encounters a record with the Bibliographic Level "a" (Monographic Component Part or "in" analytic), it looks for field 773 (Host Item Entry) from which to display the information about the host item. Since "in" analytics are a small portion of our database, it was deemed more efficient to look for this field only when the level "a" was encountered. In theory, under Format Integration, any record rightfully can carry a field 773, because all fields now are valid across all formats and, presumably, across all levels. But valid does not necessarily mean sensible. Our system probably will continue to assume that nonanalytic records will not carry a field 773, or at least not a meaningful one, and won't look for it where it is not likely to be. But other fields, like field 506 (Restrictions on Access Note), we will display without regard to the record format designated in the Leader. The system cannot know, based on the Leader codes, if a record is likely to have a field 506 note, and there is no codified way in the USMARC record to know if the note makes sense in the given context.

The Effect of Format Integration on the Union Catalog

Many OPACs are union catalogs, and these present special problems in the user interface. The user should see the union catalog as a single catalog. However, records are sent from different catalog departments that function independently. This means that the input to the union catalog can carry some variations in the treatment of identical bibliographic items. When a system displays two records rather than one, there should be a significant difference between the two; this should not occur simply because the system did not bring together two separate instances of the same work. Systems have various ways of identifying records for the same item and eliminating duplicate cataloging. The question is, will Format Integration make this more difficult?

Although I cannot be sure, I believe the answer to this is "no." Single-format items will get the same descriptive fields that they received before Format Integration, and it is these fields that are used to detect duplicates in most systems. There always has been some risk with multiformat items that they will be given radically different cataloging by different catalogers. In fact, this seems to happen rarely, and there should be no greater risk of it under Format Integration than before. At least with Format Integration, although such records may be seen as duplicates in a union catalog, catalogers will have had the opportunity to include all relevant data, regardless of the primary format chosen. It is even possible that the records might look even more alike under Format Integration.

If a union catalog keeps only one bibliographic record for each unique item, this record may be the most recent record contributed, or it may be what the system considers the "best" record. As in the changeover to AACR2 name headings, a system should give preference to a post-Format Integration record rather than a pre-Format Integration record. The post-Format Integration record might have additional fields, such as serials fields, that were not possible in the earlier cataloging. No matter how one judges which record to select, adherence to the new rules for coding USMARC fields under Format Integration should be part of the criteria. An integrated record should not be discarded for one created before Format Integration.

Probably the greatest fear for union catalogs is that some contributors will move to Format Integration faster than others, resulting in a "mixed" database. The fact is that even nonunion databases are likely to have a mix of Format Integration and pre-Format Integration records. Given the discussion above about searching and display, this should not present great problems in the user interface.

The OPAC and Quality Control

Format Integration permits the inclusion of virtually any defined field in any USMARC record. Although no one truly expects catalogers to begin adding the map scale field in music records, it may be that cataloging systems will have a hard time detecting these types of errors. Will the OPAC have to take on more responsibility for quality control?

That is a difficult question to answer now. Until we have more experience with Format Integration and more experience with how Format Integration is implemented in cataloging systems, we cannot predict the new kinds of errors we may see in incoming records. Already, the move of libraries from the national utilities, where tight quality control was the rule, to local systems that leave more to the responsibility of the individual institution, has meant that record content is not strictly by the (USMARC) book in all cases. We hope that cool heads and the librarian's innate understanding of the need for consistency will win out, and that cataloging systems will continue to enforce standards in the creation of catalog records.

Further Questions for Formats in the OPAC

Are Formats User Friendly?

The formats defined in USMARC refer only to the physical formats of materials, and this has more to do with bibliographic description than user service. Format Integration does not change this fact. For example, it does not resolve the question, "When is a map not a map?" (Answer: When it is in an atlas.) A user limiting a search to map materials will not retrieve atlases because these are considered books for the purposes of description. This distinction may not be important to the user who is interested in the information content of maps, not how they have been printed, bound, or collated. So, to begin with, formats do not relate to content.

Formats also can be confusing because the USMARC formats tend to include more than one kind of data in the concept of format. They include material type (map, projected medium), publication or collection pattern (monograph, serial), and bibliographic control (archival). Serials often are singled out for special treatment even though these are not really a format of material, but a publication pattern. Most users think of serials as simple journal publications, but a library includes many other materials under this rubric, including such commonly used works as encyclopedias and yearly fact books. Few users would put these in the same category as *Time*. OPACs often allow users to limit searches to serials, yet we know that the user's definition probably would not include a serially published video or even a monographic series.

The concept of formats lacks something that is found more readily in abstracting and indexing services: a presentation of "publication type." Some publication types are found in the subject form subfields, like "Bibliography," etc. To these, abstracting and indexing services have added forms like "general works," " research results," and "review article." Subject searching also allows access to some of the same formats that are defined in the USMARC record: maps, videorecordings, etc. It is no wonder users are confused.

Can We Really Treat All "Formats" the Same?

By unifying the USMARC formats, we are making some assumptions about the way that different sectors of the bibliographic community view their data. We already struggle with the fact that the archival community views bibliographic data with a very different eye from the nonarchival community. In some media, the concept of authorship is more varied than it is in the book world, yet the fields available are the same as the book-oriented "author" field, so all manner of responsible parties are placed in that field, such as film editors and performers in the arts. Once again, music throws a curve in its preference for uniform titles, placing its special brand of uniform titles in author/title fields that others use as synonymous to the title proper, like the 700 subfield ‡t. Thus, some fields are being used differently in different library communities. This suggests that one cannot treat all fields in all records the same, that USMARC fields take their meaning from the context of the material type being described.

The problems that arise in different treatments of fields are not related to Format Integration, but to USMARC as it is implemented currently. These fields should be scrutinized carefully, for they will lead us to areas where the USMARC format needs more work. Format Integration never was intended to resolve these problems, but it does give us a more flexible structure in which to work on new solutions.

Conclusion

Format Integration represents an evolution of the USMARC formats, not a revolution. OPAC trainers should find that Format Integration has little effect on the fundamentals of the online catalog user interface. Records that combine fields from once-distinct formats should be as readable to the user as the records in today's OPAC. Format Integration itself should require no explanatory screens or special user training sessions. If Format Integration truly is successful, the users never will know it happened.

Display of Leader, 006 Field, and 008 Field by the Utilities

(As of September 1992)

Prepared by Richard Greene

LEADER

Bytes	Element	OCLC PRISM	RLIN	WLN
00–04	Logical record length	(n/d)*	(n/d)	(n/d)
05	Record status	Rec stat	MS	(n/d)
06	Type of record	Type	BLT (combined with Leader/07)	REC TYPE
07	Bibliographic level	Bib lvl	see Leader/06	BIB LV
08	Undefined	(n/d)	(n/d)	(n/d)
09	Undefined	(n/d)	(n/d)	(n/d)
10	Indicator count	(n/d)	(n/d)	(n/d)
11	Subfield code count	(n/d)	(n/d)	(n/d)
12–16	Base address of data	(n/d)	(n/d)	(n/d)
17	Encoding level	Enc lvl	EL	ENC LV
18	Descriptive cataloging form	Desc	DCF	CAT FORM
19	Linked record requirement	(n/d)	(n/d)	(n/d)
20–23	Entry map	(n/d)	(n/d)	(n/d)

* not displayed

ALL FORMATS

008 bytes	Element	OCLC PRISM	RLIN	WLN
00–05	Date entered on file	Entered	AD	(n/d)*
06	Type of date/ publication status	Dat tp (non-serial) Pub st (serial)	PC (non-serial) PSC (serial)	DATE KY (non-serial) PUB STAT (serial)
07–10	Date 1/beginning date of publication	Dates (combined with 008/11–14)	PD (non-serial combined with 008/11–14) D (serial & mrdf ser.; combined with 008/11–14)	DATE1 (non-serial) BEG DT (serial)
11–14	Date 2/ending date of publication	see 008/07–10	see 008/07–10	DATE2 (non-serial) END DT (serial)
15–17	Place of publication, production, or execution	Ctry	CP (non-visual materials) CPR (visual materials)	CNTRY
35–37	Language	Lang	L	LAN
38	Modified record	Mod rec	MOD	MOD REC
39	Cataloging source	Source	CSC	CAT S

BOOKS

008 bytes	Element	006 bytes	OCLC PRISM	RLIN	WLN
18–21	Illustrations	01–04	Illus	ILC	ILLUS
22	Target audience	05	Int lvl	INT	INTEL LV
23	Form of item	06	Repr	REP	REPRO
24–27	Nature of contents	07–10	Cont	CON	CONTENTS
28	Government publication	11	Govt pub	GPC	GOV PUB
29	Conference publication	12	Conf pub	CPI	CONF
30	Festschrift	13	Festschr	FSI	FEST
31	Index	14	Indx	II	INDEX
32	Undefined	15	(n/d)*	(n/d)	(n/d)
33	Fiction	16	F (combined with 008/34 as F/B)	FIC	FIC
34	Biography	17	see 008/33	BIO	BIOG

* not displayed

SERIALS

008 bytes	Element	006 bytes	OCLC PRISM	RLIN	WLN
18	Frequency	01	Frequn	FRQ	FREQ
19	Regularly	02	Regulr	REG	REGLTY
20	ISDS center	03	ISDS	ISDS	ISDS
21	Type of serial	04	Ser tp	TYP	TYPE SER
22	Form of original item	05	Phys med	PHY	PHY MED
23	Form of item	06	Repr	REP	REPRO
24	Nature of entire work	07	Cont (combined with 008/25–27)	IS	TYPE MAT
25–27	Nature of contents	08–10	see 008/24	CNC	CONTENTS
28	Government publication	11	Govt pub	GPC	GOV PUB
29	Conference publication	12	Conf pub	CPI	CONF
30–32	Undefined	13–15	(n/d)*	(n/d)	(n/d)
33	Original alphabet or script of title	16	Alphabt	ALPH	ORG ALPH
34	Successive/ latest entry	17	S/L ent	SL	SL ENTRY

VISUAL MATERIALS

008 bytes	Element	006 bytes	OCLC PRISM	RLIN	WLN
18–20 s	Running time for motion pictures and video recordings	01–03	Leng	RUN	LENGTH
21	Undefined	04	(n/d)*	(n/d)	(n/d)
22	Target audience	05	Int lvl	INT	INTEL LV
23–27	Accompanying matter	06–10	Accomp	ACMP	ACC MAT
28	Government publication	11	Govt pub	GPC	GOV PUB
29–32	Undefined	12–15	(n/d)	(n/d)	(n/d)
33	Type of material	16	Type mat	TYPE	TY MAT
34	Technique	17	Tech	TEQ	TECH

* not displayed

MAPS

008 bytes	Element	006 bytes	OCLC PRISM	RLIN	WLN
18–21	Relief	01–04	Relief	RLF	RELIEF
22–24	Projection/ Prime meridian	05–07	Base	PRJ	BASE MP
25	Cartographic material type	08	RecG	GRP	REC GRP
26–27	Undefined	09–10	(n/d)*	(n/d)	(n/d)
28	Government publication	11	Govt pub	GPC	GOV PUB
29–30	Undefined	12–13	(n/d)	(n/d)	(n/d)
31	Index	14	Indx	II	INDEX
32	Undefined	15	(n/d)	(n/d)	(n/d)
33–34	Special format characteristics	16–17	Form	FMT	FORMA

MUSIC

008 bytes	Element	006 bytes	OCLC PRISM	RLIN	WLN
18–19	Form of composition	01–02	Comp	FCP	COMP
20	Format of music	03	Format	SCO (scores only)	SCORE
21	Undefined	04	(n/d)*	(n/d)	(n/d)
22	Target audience	05	Int lvl	INT	INTEL LV
23	Form of item	06	Repr	REP (scores only)	REPRO
24–29	Accompanying matter	07–12	Accomp	AMC	ACC MAT
30–31	Literary text for sound recordings	13–14	LTxt	LIT (sound recordings only)	LIT TEXT
31–34	Undefined	15–17	(n/d)	(n/d)	(n/d)

COMPUTER FILES

008 bytes	Element	006 bytes	OCLC PRISM	RLIN	WLN
18–21	Undefined	01–04	(n/d)*	(n/d)	(n/d)
22	Target audience	05	Audience	AUD	INTEL LV
23–25	Undefined	06–08	(n/d)	(n/d)	(n/d)
26	Type of computer file	09	File	TMDF	TYP FILE
27	Undefined	10	(n/d)	(n/d)	(n/d)
28	Government publication	11	Govt pub	GPC	GOV PUB
29–34	Undefined	12–17	(n/d)	(n/d)	(n/d)

* not displayed

Glossary and Acronyms
Used in This Volume

006 field A new fixed field similar to the 008 field, added to the USMARC
format as a part of Format Integration, in which additional characteristics of the item can be coded. See the appendix for the display of data
from the 006 field in the three utilities' systems.

008 field A fixed field giving coded data generally descriptive of the item
being cataloged. See the appendix for the display of data from the 008
field in the three utilities' systems.

AACR2 Anglo-American Cataloguing Rules, second edition.

ALA American Library Association

ALCTS Association for Library Collections & Technical Services, a
division of the American Library Association; formerly Resources and
Technical Services Division (RTSD).

AMC Archival and Manuscripts Control format of the USMARC formats.

bibliographic formats Under the current implementation of USMARC, a
series of seven documents composing the Books, Archival and Manuscripts Control, Computer Files, Maps, Music, Visual Materials, and

Serials formats. After Format Integration, these will be combined into a single format.

Bibliographic Level A byte in the Leader that indicates that the item being cataloged is a monograph, serial, collection, or a part thereof. See the appendix for the display of data from this byte in the three utilities' systems.

byte A character position in the fixed-length fields such as the Leader, 006 field, and 008 field. Bytes are numbered from the beginning of the field starting with number 0. See the appendix for the display of data from the Leader, 006 field, and 008 field in the three utilities' systems.

coding See **tagging.**

content designators MARC tags, subfields, and other coding in the MARC record.

fixed field A field in the MARC record comprising fixed-length data used for machine processing. See also **byte.** See the appendix for the display of data from the Leader, 006 field, and 008 field in the three utilities' systems.

Leader A fixed field at the beginning of the MARC record generally giving information needed for the machine processing of the record.

LITA Library and Information Technology Association, a division of the American Library Association.

MARBI The Machine-Readable Bibliographic Information Committee, an interdivisional committee of the Association for Library Collections & Technical Services, the Library and Information Technology Association, and the Reference and Adult Services Division. This committee and representatives from the utilities and associations representing cataloging interests make up the USMARC Advisory Group that advises the Library of Congress on changes to the USMARC format.

MARC MAchine-Readable Cataloging. The record format, based on the American National Standards Institute standard Z39.2, that forms the basis for the various national implementations, such as USMARC, AUSMARC, CANMARC, and UKMARC.

OCLC OCLC Online Computer Library Center.

OPAC Online Public Access Catalog.

RASD Reference and Adult Services Division of the American Library Association.

RLIN Research Libraries Information Network of the Research Libraries Group (RLG).

RTSD Resources and Technical Services Division of the American Library Association; now the Association for Library Collections & Technical Services (ALCTS).

tagging The process of assigning tags and subfield coding to bibliographic data and completing information in the fixed fields.

Type of Record A byte in the Leader that specifies the material characteristics of the item being cataloged. Before Format Integration, this byte determined the format for use in cataloging the item. See the appendix for the display of this byte in the three utilities' systems.

USMARC The United States implementation of the MARC format, including the definition of content designators.

utilities The major bibliographic databases and cataloging systems, here referring generally to OCLC, RLIN, and WLN.

validation tables Lists of valid USMARC tags often carried in library automation systems. These tables are used to check records during editing or loading to ensure that tagging is valid.

variable data fields Fields in a MARC record that can vary in length, depending upon the type of data included in it—e.g., author, title, physical description.

WLN Western (formerly Washington) Library Network.

Index

Individual fields in the MARC format are indexed in a separate index following the main index

Index of MARC Fields